# FORAGING
# PENNSYLVANIA AND
# NEW JERSEY

# HELP US KEEP THIS GUIDE UP TO DATE

Every effort has been made by the author and editors to make this guide as accurate and useful as possible. However, many things can change after a guide is published—regulations change, techniques evolve, facilities come under new management, etc.

We appreciate hearing from you concerning your experiences with this guide and how you feel it could be improved and kept up to date. While we may not be able to respond to all comments and suggestions, we'll take them to heart and we'll also make certain to share them with the author. Please send your comments and suggestions to the following address:

FalconGuides
Reader Response/Editorial Department
246 Goose Lane, Suite 200
Guilford, CT 06437

Thanks for your input!

# FORAGING PENNSYLVANIA AND NEW JERSEY

Finding, Identifying, and Preparing Edible Wild Foods

## Debbie Naha-Koretzky

GUILFORD, CONNECTICUT

# FALCONGUIDES®

An imprint of The Rowman & Littlefield Publishing Group, Inc.
4501 Forbes Blvd., Ste. 200
Lanham, MD 20706
www.rowman.com

Falcon and FalconGuides are registered trademarks and Make Adventure Your Story is a trademark of The Rowman & Littlefield Publishing Group, Inc.

Distributed by NATIONAL BOOK NETWORK

All photos by Debbie Naha-Koretzky with the exception of:
Pg. xvii photo courtesy of Maia Stern
Pgs. 100, 101, 102, photos courtesy of Karen Carlough

Maps by The Rowman & Littlefield Publishing Group, Inc.

British Library Cataloguing-in-Publication Information available

**Library of Congress Cataloging in Publication Data**

Names: Naha-Koretzky, Debbie, 1955- author.
Title: Foraging Pennsylvania and New Jersey : finding, identifying, and
  preparing edible wild foods / Debbie Naha-Koretzky.
Description: Guilford, Connecticut : FalconGuides, 2021. | Includes
  bibliographical references and index. | Summary: "From cattails to wild
  garlic, this guide uncovers the edible wild foods and healthful herbs of
  Pennsylvania and New Jersey"— Provided by publisher.
Identifiers: LCCN 2020049661 (print) | LCCN 2020049662 (ebook) | ISBN
  9781493056279 (trade paperback) | ISBN 9781493056286 (epub)
Subjects: LCSH: Wild plants, Edible—Pennsylvania—Identification. | Wild
  plants, Edible—New Jersey—Identification. | Plants,
  Edible—Pennsylvania—Identification. | Plants, Edible—New
  Jersey—Identification.
Classification: LCC QK98.5.U6 N35 2021  (print) | LCC QK98.5.U6  (ebook) |
  DDC 581.6/3209748—dc23
LC record available at https://lccn.loc.gov/2020049661
LC ebook record available at https://lccn.loc.gov/2020049662

♾™  The paper used in this publication meets the minimum requirements of American National Standard for Information Sciences—Permanence of Paper for Printed Library Materials, ANSI/NISO Z39.48-1992.

This book is a work of reference. Readers should always consult an expert before using any foraged item. The author, editors, and publisher of this work have checked with sources believed to be reliable in their efforts to confirm the accuracy and completeness of the information presented herein and that the information is in accordance with the standard practices accepted at the time of publication. However, neither the author, editors, and publisher nor any other party involved in the creation and publication of this work warrant that the information is in every respect accurate and complete, and they are not responsible for errors or omissions or for any consequences from the application of the information in this book. In light of ongoing research and changes in clinical experience and in governmental regulations, readers are encouraged to confirm the information contained herein with additional sources. This book does not purport to be a complete presentation of all plants, and the genera, species, and cultivars discussed or pictured herein are but a small fraction of the plants found in the wild, in an urban or suburban landscape, or in a home. Given the global movement of plants, we would expect continual introduction of species having toxic properties to the regions discussed in this book. We have made every attempt to be botanically accurate, but regional variations in plant names, growing conditions, and availability may affect the accuracy of the information provided. A positive identification of an individual plant is most likely when a freshly collected part of the plant containing leaves and flowers or fruits is presented to a knowledgeable botanist or horticulturist. Poison Control Centers generally have relationships with the botanical community should the need for plant identification arise. We have attempted to provide accurate descriptions of plants, but there is no substitute for direct interaction with a trained botanist or horticulturist for plant identification.

**In cases of exposure or ingestion, contact a Poison Control Center (800-222-1222), a medical toxicologist, another appropriate health-care provider, or an appropriate reference resource.**

*For Henry*

# CONTENTS

Preface . . . . . . . . . . . . . . . . . . . . . . . . . . . . . . . . . . . . . . . . . xiv

Introduction . . . . . . . . . . . . . . . . . . . . . . . . . . . . . . . . . . . . . . xvi
    Why Do We Forage? . . . . . . . . . . . . . . . . . . . . . . . . . . . . . . . xvi
    Safety . . . . . . . . . . . . . . . . . . . . . . . . . . . . . . . . . . . . . . . xvi
    Nutrition from the Wild . . . . . . . . . . . . . . . . . . . . . . . . . . . . xviii
    Responsible Foraging . . . . . . . . . . . . . . . . . . . . . . . . . . . . . . xix
    A Word on Mushrooms . . . . . . . . . . . . . . . . . . . . . . . . . . . . . xix
    A Forager's Tools . . . . . . . . . . . . . . . . . . . . . . . . . . . . . . . . . xx
    How to Use This Book . . . . . . . . . . . . . . . . . . . . . . . . . . . . . . xx

Plants of Spring . . . . . . . . . . . . . . . . . . . . . . . . . . . . . . . . . . . . . 1
    Black Locust   *Robinia pseudoacacia* . . . . . . . . . . . . . . . . . . . 2
    Cattail   *Typha* spp. . . . . . . . . . . . . . . . . . . . . . . . . . . . . . 5
    Chickweed   *Stellaria media* . . . . . . . . . . . . . . . . . . . . . . . . 9
    Chicory   *Cichorium intybus* . . . . . . . . . . . . . . . . . . . . . . . 12
    Cleavers   *Galium aparine* . . . . . . . . . . . . . . . . . . . . . . . . 16
    Curly Dock   *Rumex crispus* . . . . . . . . . . . . . . . . . . . . . . . 19
    Dame's Rocket   *Hesperis matronalis* . . . . . . . . . . . . . . . . . . 23
    Dandelion   *Taraxacum officinale* . . . . . . . . . . . . . . . . . . . . 26
    Eastern White Pine   *Pinus strobus* . . . . . . . . . . . . . . . . . . . 30
    Garlic Mustard   *Alliaria petiolata* . . . . . . . . . . . . . . . . . . . 34
    Greenbrier   *Smilax rotundifolia* . . . . . . . . . . . . . . . . . . . . 38
    Hairy Bittercress   *Cardamine hirsuta* . . . . . . . . . . . . . . . . . 42
    Henbit   *Lamium amplexicaule* . . . . . . . . . . . . . . . . . . . . . 46
    Japanese Knotweed   *Polygonum cuspidatum* . . . . . . . . . . . . . 49
    Maple   *Acer* spp. . . . . . . . . . . . . . . . . . . . . . . . . . . . . . . 53
    Ostrich Fern   *Matteuccia struthiopteris* . . . . . . . . . . . . . . . . 56
    Plantain   *Plantago* spp. . . . . . . . . . . . . . . . . . . . . . . . . . 60
    Purple Deadnettle   *Lamium purpureum* . . . . . . . . . . . . . . . . 64
    Ramps   *Allium tricoccum* . . . . . . . . . . . . . . . . . . . . . . . . 68
    Redbud   *Cercis canadensis* . . . . . . . . . . . . . . . . . . . . . . . 72
    Spring Beauty   *Claytonia virginica* . . . . . . . . . . . . . . . . . . . 75
    Spruce   *Picea* spp. . . . . . . . . . . . . . . . . . . . . . . . . . . . . . 79
    Stinging Nettle   *Urtica dioica* . . . . . . . . . . . . . . . . . . . . . 82
    Trout Lily   *Erythronium americanum* . . . . . . . . . . . . . . . . . 86
    Violets   *Viola* spp. . . . . . . . . . . . . . . . . . . . . . . . . . . . . . 89

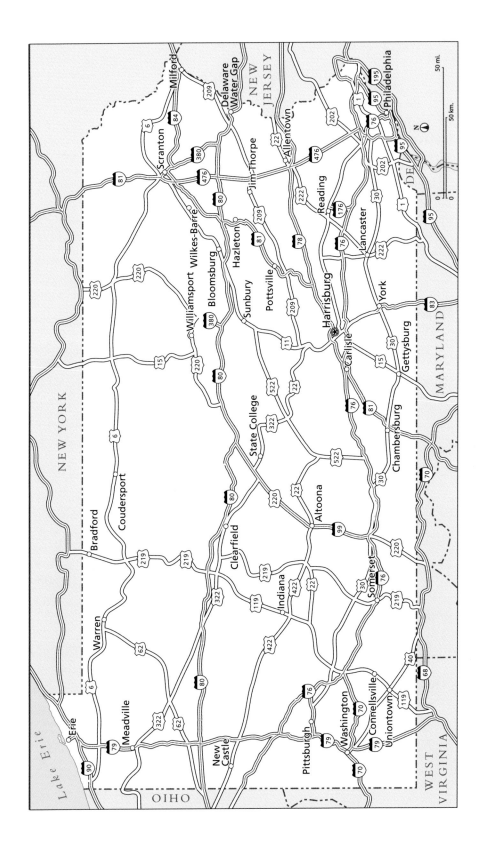

Wild Garlic   *Allium vineale* . . . . . . . . . . . . . . . . . . . . . . . . . . . . 92
Wintercress   *Barbarea vulgaris* . . . . . . . . . . . . . . . . . . . . . . . 96

## Plants of Summer . . . . . . . . . . . . . . . . . . . . . . . . . . . . . . . . . .99
Beach Plum   *Prunus maritima* . . . . . . . . . . . . . . . . . . . . . . . 100
Black Cherry   *Prunus serotina* . . . . . . . . . . . . . . . . . . . . . . . 103
Blueberry   *Vaccinium* spp. . . . . . . . . . . . . . . . . . . . . . . . . . 106
Brambles   *Rubus* spp. . . . . . . . . . . . . . . . . . . . . . . . . . . . . 109
Common Milkweed   *Asclepias syriaca* . . . . . . . . . . . . . . . . . . 112
Cornelian Cherry   *Cornus mas* . . . . . . . . . . . . . . . . . . . . . . . 116
Elderberry   *Sambucus canadensis* and *S. nigra* . . . . . . . . . . . . . 119
Heal-All   *Prunella vulgaris* . . . . . . . . . . . . . . . . . . . . . . . . . 122
Lamb's-quarter   *Chenopodium album* . . . . . . . . . . . . . . . . . . 125
Mayapple   *Podophyllum peltatum* . . . . . . . . . . . . . . . . . . . . . 128
Mulberry   *Morus alba* and *M. rubra* . . . . . . . . . . . . . . . . . . . 131
Oxeye Daisy   *Leucanthemum vulgare* . . . . . . . . . . . . . . . . . . . 135
Purslane   *Portulaca oleracea* . . . . . . . . . . . . . . . . . . . . . . . . 138
Queen Anne's Lace / Wild Carrot   *Daucus carota* . . . . . . . . . . . . 141
Serviceberry   *Amelanchier* spp. . . . . . . . . . . . . . . . . . . . . . . 145
Spearmint   *Mentha spicata* . . . . . . . . . . . . . . . . . . . . . . . . . 148
Strawberry / Wild Strawberry   *Fragaria virginiana* . . . . . . . . . . . 151
Watercress   *Nasturtium officinale* . . . . . . . . . . . . . . . . . . . . . 154
Wood Sorrel   *Oxalis stricta* . . . . . . . . . . . . . . . . . . . . . . . . . 157

## Plants of Fall . . . . . . . . . . . . . . . . . . . . . . . . . . . . . . . . . . . .160
Autumn Olive   *Elaeagnus umbellata* . . . . . . . . . . . . . . . . . . . 161
Beech   *Fagus grandifolia* . . . . . . . . . . . . . . . . . . . . . . . . . . . 164
Black Walnut   *Juglans nigra* . . . . . . . . . . . . . . . . . . . . . . . . 168
Burdock   *Arctium minus* and *A. lappa* . . . . . . . . . . . . . . . . . . 172
Ginkgo   *Ginkgo biloba* . . . . . . . . . . . . . . . . . . . . . . . . . . . . 175
Grape / Wild Grape   *Vitis* spp. . . . . . . . . . . . . . . . . . . . . . . . 179
Ground Cherry   *Physalis* spp. . . . . . . . . . . . . . . . . . . . . . . . . 183
Hackberry   *Celtis* spp. . . . . . . . . . . . . . . . . . . . . . . . . . . . . 186
Hawthorn   *Crataegus* spp. . . . . . . . . . . . . . . . . . . . . . . . . . . 189
Oak / Acorn   *Quercus* spp. . . . . . . . . . . . . . . . . . . . . . . . . . 193
Partridge Berry   *Mitchella repens* . . . . . . . . . . . . . . . . . . . . . 197
Pawpaw   *Asimina triloba* . . . . . . . . . . . . . . . . . . . . . . . . . . 200
Persimmon   *Diospyros virginiana* . . . . . . . . . . . . . . . . . . . . . 203
Rose   *Rosa* spp. . . . . . . . . . . . . . . . . . . . . . . . . . . . . . . . . 206
Spicebush   *Lindera benzoin* . . . . . . . . . . . . . . . . . . . . . . . . . 210
Staghorn Sumac   *Rhus typhina* . . . . . . . . . . . . . . . . . . . . . . . 213
Wintergreen   *Gaultheria procumbens* . . . . . . . . . . . . . . . . . . . 217

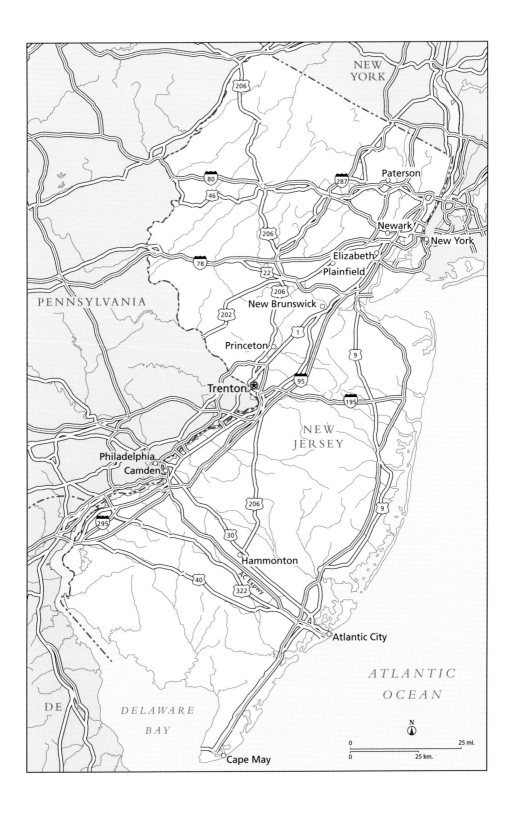

NEW YORK

PENNSYLVANIA

NEW JERSEY

206

80

46

287

Paterson

Newark

New York

206

78

Elizabeth

22

Plainfield

206

New Brunswick

202

1

Princeton

9

95

Trenton

195

Philadelphia

Camden

206

295

9

30

Hammonton

40

AC Expwy

322

Atlantic City

DE

DELAWARE
BAY

ATLANTIC

OCEAN

N

0        25 mi.
0        25 km.

Cape May

**Mushrooms** . . . . . . . . . . . . . . . . . . . . . . . . . . . . . . . . . . . .**221**
   Chanterelles   *Cantharellus* spp.. . . . . . . . . . . . . . . . . . . . . . 222
   Chicken of the Woods   *Laetiporus sulphureus* . . . . . . . . . . . . . . 226
   Giant Puffball   *Calvatia gigantea* . . . . . . . . . . . . . . . . . . . . 230
   Hen of the Woods   *Grifola frondosa*. . . . . . . . . . . . . . . . . . . 233
   Lion's Mane   *Hericium erinaceus* . . . . . . . . . . . . . . . . . . . . 236
   Morels   *Morchella* spp. . . . . . . . . . . . . . . . . . . . . . . . . . . . 239
   Pheasant's Back   *Polyporus squamosus* . . . . . . . . . . . . . . . . . 244

**Bibliography** . . . . . . . . . . . . . . . . . . . . . . . . . . . . . . . . . . . .**248**

**Glossary** . . . . . . . . . . . . . . . . . . . . . . . . . . . . . . . . . . . . . . .**268**

**Index** . . . . . . . . . . . . . . . . . . . . . . . . . . . . . . . . . . . . . . . . .**271**

# PREFACE

Dandelions were my gateway plant into foraging.

My interest in plants began as an inner-city kid, growing up across the river from New York City. I grew up in Union City, New Jersey, the most densely populated city in the United States.

I was not exactly surrounded by greenery. I remember wanting to know the names of the weeds that grew in my neighborhood, sprouting up in patches of dirt and cracks in the concrete. Although I did not know their names back then, I was fascinated with Asiatic dayflower, galinsoga, and dandelions.

While working on my undergraduate degree in biology at what is now New Jersey City University, someone told me you could eat the dandelions on the campus lawn. Well, that was it. That spark ignited my passion. I wanted to know everything I could about wild edible plants.

I went on to receive a master's in clinical nutrition from New York University. Over the years I worked as a nutritionist for several institutions in NYC and as a dietitian supervisor at New York Downtown Hospital.

I always wanted to know what was "out there" in nature that is food for humans. Our species has become so disconnected from wild foods we were designed to eat. Cultivated plants have much of their innate goodness bred out of them to achieve higher yields, uniform size, sweeter fruits, and milder tasting greens. Wild food is so underappreciated.

I've conducted hundreds of foraging walks and programs for various organizations, environmental centers, native plant societies, state parks, etc. Presentations are usually followed by a foraging walk, wherever we happen to be. I remind people that you can find wild food everywhere. And I love doing wild food demos! I take pride in providing accurate, evidence-based information to people. And that's exactly what this book offers.

One good thing about reaching a certain age is that you've got lots of experience behind you. In addition to being a licensed dietitian nutritionist, I'm also a certified science teacher, a member of the Association of Foragers, and a Pennsylvania Master Naturalist. In New Jersey, I worked at the Great Swamp in Morris County as a naturalist. In 2009 and 2010 I was presented with the US President's Volunteer Service Award for work as a certified Rutgers Master Gardener. I like to think that my training in nutrition combined with this assortment of life experiences gives me a unique approach to wild edible plants.

I'm very glad to have the chance to produce this book. I would like to thank FalconGuides for their advocacy of foraging, and for their flexibility and assistance in shaping this book. Sincere gratitude goes out to my editor, Katie O'Dell, for her enthusiasm, support, endless patience with my questions, and for helping this project come to life. Enormous thanks to Laura Foord and Sacha Forgoston for their friendship, generous spirit, and invaluable assistance. And to Henry. This book would never have been possible without your loving support.

# INTRODUCTION

## Why Do We Forage?

Foraging, the act of searching for and gathering wild food, takes us back to our prehistoric roots.

Humans evolved as hunter-gatherers. The "gatherer" part was vital to our survival, as wild plants provided necessary nutrition. Nowadays most of us don't need to forage for survival. Even enthusiastic foragers don't subsist entirely on wild food but use their foraged finds to supplement a regular diet.

I like hearing why people are interesting in foraging. I get many different answers when I ask. Responses include having a local food source, free food, connection to nature, superior nutrition, something fun to do with the kids, food security (food availability in survival situations), and experiencing something new.

As a nutritionist, I've always been interested in knowing what nourishment is out there in the wild. There is something satisfying about knowing there is food available. Even in winter, you can obtain nutrients. Bringing home even a small part of a meal that did not come from a supermarket brings me satisfaction. It provides a grounding connection to the environment.

Regardless of your reason for wanting to forage, it's a valuable, nourishing, healthful skill to cultivate. I hope this book can help.

## Safety

If you are a beginning forager, I recommend starting with plants that grow close to home. Unless you go overboard with weeding and herbicide use, you're likely to have a good amount of wild food right in your backyard.

Dandelion is a perfect first plant to learn. It is widely available, easy to recognize, the entire plant is edible, and there are no problematic look-alikes. Starting with a relatively safe plant is especially helpful when teaching the fundamentals of foraging to children.

Foraging together teaches children nature appreciation, ecology, seasonal changes, and more. It strengthens their understanding of the natural world. **Caution:** Children should be instructed to never eat anything without a parent present.

Positive plant identification is essential. Read the entire description for any plant you are planning to eat. If it "almost" fits, that's not enough. Obtain at least a few field guides. Cross-check various sources to determine accuracy. And don't believe everything you read online. Be careful of myths. Time and time again I hear things like "If an animal eats it, you can too." That one can really get you

Dandelions are a perfect introduction to the wonders of nature. MAIA STERN

into trouble. If at all possible, learn from an experienced forager. There's nothing like meeting a plant in its natural habitat. A photo in a book doesn't compare.

Learn which parts of a plant are safe to use, and if they need to be cooked or prepared in any particular way. Some fruits are safe only when ripe. Some seeds need to be avoided.

If you don't already know, learn what poison ivy looks like. Steer clear of any area that may have been sprayed with pesticides or herbicides. Avoid busy roads, ditches, railroads, contaminated waters, or any area that doesn't look right, even if the plants look healthy.

While look-alike plants never look exactly alike, sometimes the differences are subtle. Get to know your plant. And be careful with common plant names. Sometimes a common name can refer to more than one plant. For example, hemlock. If someone talks about making a vitamin C–rich tea from hemlock, make sure they're referring to the hemlock tree (*Tsuga canadensis*) and not the deadly poisonous hemlock plant (*Conium maculatum*). Check for scientific names when needed.

Always start with a small amount of any new food to check for tolerance. You can be allergic to any food, even from a grocery store.

Learning about foraging doesn't have to be scary. Just learn everything you can about your plant until you feel confident enough to give it a try.

## Nutrition from the Wild

The Mediterranean diet is globally known to be one of the healthiest diets. Based on foods eaten in countries around the Mediterranean Sea, it focuses on eating lots of vegetables, whole fruits, beans, nuts, whole grains, seafood, and olive oil. Meat is consumed sparingly. Research shows that this lifestyle may help prevent heart disease, type 2 diabetes, cognitive decline, obesity, and certain cancers, and may increase longevity.

One often overlooked but significant aspect of this traditional diet is the regular use of wild foraged greens. In Greece and other Mediterranean countries, foraging and eating wild plants has been practiced for centuries.

In general, wild plants offer more nutrition than conventionally grown crops, with higher levels of vitamins, minerals, and antioxidants. Increased intake of wild foods would certainly be conducive to better health. We would do well to eat more of them.

As a professional nutritionist, I would be remiss if I did not include a few more dietary tips:

- Eating healthy doesn't equal deprivation. Sweets in moderation, not too much salt, and eat just as many calories as your body needs to maintain a healthy weight (easier said than done, I know). A largely plant-based (not necessarily vegetarian) diet is probably best.
- Protein requirements can be met without eating meat. Beans, lentils, soy products, seeds, nuts, and nut butters are excellent protein sources.
- When eating animal products, keep in mind that the composition of meat, eggs, milk, and butter is highly influenced by what the animal ate.
- Mass-produced beef is from cows fattened on grains. Grass-fed beef is from cows that eat mostly grass. The meat of grass-fed animals contains significantly more antioxidants than the meat of grain-fed animals, and much higher levels of beneficial omega-3 fatty acids.
- Milk and butter from grass-fed cows have healthier fat profiles and higher amounts of beta-carotene, an important antioxidant.
- The most nutritious eggs you can buy are pastured eggs. They are laid by hens that have free access to sun, fresh air, and a diet of plants and insects, along with some regular feed.
- Choose foods that have most of their original nutrients intact. Whole-grain products are superior to refined flour. Whole fruits contain many nutrients and dietary fiber and are significantly better than fruit juices which can cause unhealthy fluctuations in blood sugar levels.

- Hydration is important for overall health. Drink lots of water.
- Eat fresh fruits and plenty of vegetables, some of them wild!

## Responsible Foraging

Some of the best foraging can be done in your own backyard. Many volunteer plants, aka "weeds," are some of the best wild foods available.

When you do venture out from your home base, be aware of foraging etiquette and other restrictions regarding collecting. As tempting as those big chicken mushrooms on someone's old oak can be, knock on the door first and ask.

Check for local or county regulations. It is fairly common to see signs in parks that spell out rules, including those regarding picking or foraging.

In New Jersey state parks, foraging is not permitted according to the Administrative Code, which states that unless permission is obtained, "A person shall not abuse, mutilate, injure, destroy, move or remove any plant or animal or natural resource."

In Pennsylvania state forests and parks, the gathering of edible wild plants or plant parts—fruits, nuts, berries, and fungi—in reasonable amounts is permitted as long as it is for personal or family consumption. And as always, if a species is rare or threatened in any way, it should not be removed or harmed.

At every foraging program I do, I advocate responsible and sustainable harvesting. Overharvesting of plants often results in decimated populations. For example, see the "Ramps" entry. Even when plants are plentiful, take just what you need. Don't destroy roots if you are only using the aboveground parts. And where permitted, harvest invasive species to your heart's content.

## A Word on Mushrooms

You may have heard of the "foolproof four" (or five, or whatever number), referring to the edible mushroom species that are easiest to identify. The list can vary, but it usually includes morels, chanterelles, chicken of the woods, and giant puffballs. Other mushrooms that sometimes make "the list" are lion's mane, pheasant's back, and hen of the woods. You will find all of these in this book. They are species with easily identifiable characteristics, and, with reasonable care taken, there should be no problem with identification.

Begin with the more foolproof species and get to know each one well enough to be absolutely certain of its identity. Don't rely on one person or book to identify mushrooms you are planning to eat. Contact your local mushroom club for educational events and foraging forays. Find an expert forager to get you started.

There are some common (and dangerous) myths surrounding mushrooms. An example is that a poisonous mushroom will turn a silver spoon black. There is no quick and easy shortcut to tell a poisonous mushroom from a safe one.

You need to be able to identify each mushroom before you eat it. In the field, it can help to have a small mirror on hand to look underneath a cap (to identify pores versus gills, for example). Buy a few good field guides. Be meticulous about identification. As with plants, check every detail and be 100 percent certain of identity.

And remember: All mushrooms should be cooked before eating.

## A Forager's Tools

Foraging doesn't require specialized or fancy tools.

What you need depends on what you're harvesting. For example, if you're looking for stinging nettles, you would bring appropriate gloves, a bag or two, and snippers. Bring a digging tool if you're going for roots. Shallow boxes or containers are good to transport fragile fruits like pawpaws or persimmons securely in a single layer. It's always good to have some bags with you. You might wind up taking home a haul of black walnuts or a giant puffball.

For general comfort and safety, take along bug repellent, water, food, weather-appropriate clothing, and a cell phone.

## How to Use This Book

The plants in this book are grouped by season. Some plants don't fit neatly into one season and are placed in the season when the first edible parts appear or the season in which the plant is most useful. The mushroom section follows the plants section.

Each plant and mushroom has a "real" or scientific name, which is included in italics. Clear information for positive identification is given and backed up by photos to illustrate specific characteristics. Problematic look-alike species are described in detail.

When health-related or nutritional information is presented, it is done with a great deal of caution. As a health professional, I have always respected the value of research-based information.

Journal articles, books, and other publications that provide nutrition analysis and other such information are listed in the bibliography. Take a peek back there. Even if you aren't planning to read the research, it will give you some idea of the science that supports the information presented in this book.

Traditional uses of plants are covered. Sometimes scientific research actually supports popular health claims. Often there has not been much research done, and all we have are anecdotes.

Edibility of a plant is occasionally a matter of debate. I always err on the side of caution.

The species presented are found in the Pennsylvania / New Jersey area and, in most cases, beyond.

The recipes in this book are basic, involving simple ingredients and minimal preparation. They may not be fancy or terribly innovative, but they are wholesome, with clear instructions that provide a feel for using foraged foods. Feel free to make ingredient substitutions.

# Plants of Spring

Black locust blossoms are sweet smelling and a culinary delight.

## BLACK LOCUST
*Robinia pseudoacacia*

**Family:** Fabaceae
**Also called:** Robinia, yellow locust, false acacia
**Uses:** Only the flowers are edible; raw or cooked into fritters, brewed as a tea, etc.
**Cautions:** Leaves, twigs, seedpods, bark, wood, and root are toxic. No look-alike trees.
**Season:** Spring
**Range:** Throughout New Jersey and Pennsylvania; found in floodplains, thickets, roadsides, forest edges
**Description:** Deciduous tree. Fragrant white flowers hanging in showy panicles appear in spring, each flower about 1" long. Leaves are 7"–18" long, alternate, pinnately compound with odd number of leaflets; margins are smooth. Fruit is a thin, flat pod, 2"–5" long. Twigs have paired sharp spines, which may be absent in mature trees. Brown bark is deeply furrowed.

Available for a short time in late spring, black locust blossoms are a treat for the senses. Hanging in white pendulous clusters, the sweet-smelling blooms are a short-lived culinary delicacy. Their fresh floral taste reminds me of sweet peas in flower form.

The blooms can be enjoyed straight from the tree or used in any number of ways. Add them to fruit salad, garnish a cake, fold into custard, or steep in boiled water for a fragrant tea. Black locust flowers are commonly made into fritters. Simply combine with a thin pancake batter and fry.

Black locust flowers make tasty fritters.

You have about two weeks in May to experience this fleeting pleasure. A tree in bloom will typically bear abundantly. The flowers can be frozen, but with some loss of quality. The blooms are the only part of the tree you can eat. Debate exists about the edibility of black locust seeds, so stick with the flowers. There are reports of children being poisoned by chewing the leaves, seeds, or inner bark. The exotic-looking flowers are a source of natural antioxidants. They offer the benefits of flavonoids, phenolic compounds, vitamin C, and protein, and are rich in copper, calcium, and chromium.

The genus name *Robinia* is for the French botanist Jean Robin, who first cultivated the tree in Europe. *Pseudoacacia* translates to "false acacia." True acacia trees are another group in the same family. Black locust's native range is considered to be central Pennsylvania south through the Appalachians to Alabama. The species has been widely planted and is naturalized around the world.

The wood is favored for being hard, strong, and rot resistant when in contact with soil. It is good for making fence posts, tool handles, railroad ties, and furniture. Native Americans cultivated the tree as a source of wood to make hunting bows. Black locust is also prized as firewood, since it burns slowly and has a high heat content.

Black locust flowers are tasty and rich in nutrients.

The flowers are an early source of nectar and pollen for bees. Honey made from the nectar is very light colored and delicate in flavor. The species is widely planted in Europe for this purpose, and the product is known as acacia honey.

RECIPE

**Black Locust Pea Salad**

1 pound frozen green peas, rinsed in cool water and drained
¼ cup chopped red onion
½ cup thinly sliced radish
2 ounces cheddar cheese, cubed
2 tablespoons white wine vinegar
¼–⅓ cup mayonnaise
1½ cups black locust flowers, stripped from main stem (a few reserved for garnish)

In a large bowl, toss the peas, red onion, radishes, and cheese together. Stir in the vinegar and mayonnaise. Gently fold in the flowers. Garnish with reserved flowers. Cover and refrigerate until chilled. Will keep 2–3 days refrigerated.

Cattails are the "supermarket of the swamp."

## CATTAIL
*Typha* spp.

**Family:** Typhaceae
**Also called:** Common cattail, bulrush, punks, Cossack asparagus, cat o' nine tails
**Uses:** Rhizomes, shoots, pollen, and flower spikes; raw or cooked
**Cautions:** Possible look-alike species; polluted areas
**Season:** Year-round
**Range:** Throughout New Jersey and Pennsylvania; wetlands, swamps, marshes, ditches; full sun
**Description:** Reedy plant up to 9' tall. Long, strap-like leaves. Flowering stalk a cylindrical spike with male portion above female, each consisting of tiny, tightly packed flowers. Male spike develops yellow pollen. Female is brown when fertilized, expands into a fluffy seed head. Root is a thick white rhizome.

Frequently referred to as the "supermarket of the swamp," cattails have definitely earned the nickname. The plant is a year-round food source offering a variety of edible parts.

The young shoots in spring are a tasty vegetable. Immature flower spikes and pollen provide nourishment, and the roots can be gathered year-round to provide complex carbohydrates. The common native species, *T. latifolia*, was an

New green cattail shoots

important plant to Native Americans. Various parts were eaten, and the plant was made into mats, baskets, and shelter. Seed head fluff was used as stuffing for diapers and pillows.

The first food cattails offer foragers is their tender young shoots in spring. Also known as cattail hearts, the creamy white section of the lower stem tastes like crunchy cucumber. To harvest, identify young cattails by looking for the old growth and tattered seed heads of last year's plants. Here you should find the new green growth.

Grasp the inner leaves near the base, and pull straight up. The leaves will separate from the rhizome, which stays in the mud. The lower 4–5 inches of the stem are tender. Peel away any tough layers. Cut off the green upper parts. Prepare as you would asparagus.

The green flower spikes can be eaten in spring. Roasted or boiled, they are described as tasting like corn. The male, upper part of the spike will develop protein-rich pollen. To collect, place a bag or container over the spike and shake. Add the yellow powder to pancake batter, soups, or casseroles for a protein boost.

The lower female section becomes fertilized and turns into the familiar brown "corn dog" or "hot-dog-on-a-stick," the iconic cattail image associated with swamps. After fertilization, the male part withers away to a thin vestige.

Each autumn, cattails store starch in their roots for next spring's growth. The best time to forage them is at this time, although they are harvestable year-round. Use a shovel to dig them out. If growing in water, use your hands to find them. Follow the plant down until you can feel the horizontal rhizome off to one side. Wiggle and pull until it loosens. Use a knife to separate the rhizome from

**Simple Cattail Shoots**

Place trimmed cattail shoots in a saucepan and add water just to cover. Simmer for about 5 minutes or until tender/crisp. Drain. Serve with salt, pepper, and butter to taste.

the stalk. You may find pointed little corms sprouting from a rhizome. These can be eaten too. There is no poisonous part to the plant.

The rhizomes can be boiled or baked. You'll need to remove the thick fibers as you eat the starchy parts. Starchy flour can be isolated from rhizomes by crushing them underwater. The starchy slurry produced can be used to thicken soups. The pollen, as well as all other parts of the plant, are rich in protein. Cattail shoots are a source of iron, calcium, magnesium, and vitamin K.

In the 1940s, Syracuse University conducted research showing that 140 tons of cattail rhizomes could be harvested per acre, ten times the average yield of potatoes. When harvesting, make sure to harvest from "clean" areas. Cattails are good at taking up bad things. They accumulate pollutants including arsenic, cadmium, and lead. In fact, cattail species are often used in bioremediation efforts to clean up toxic industrial waste sites.

The fertilized female "corn dog"

The two species most often found in the area are common cattail (*T. latifolia*), which is native, and narrowleaf cattail (*T. angustifolia*), introduced from Europe. A hybrid of the two is *Typha x glauca*. To foragers they are used interchangeably.

In their young stages, cattail and iris leaves may look similar. To be certain you have cattails, look for the old brown seed heads. The iris does not have this seed head. Also, iris stems are flattened at the base or fan shaped. Cattail stems are round or oval and do not form a fan at the base. Iris is toxic if eaten.

Pollen-rich male section on top, green female spike below

Open-faced hummus with chickweed

## CHICKWEED
*Stellaria media*

**Family:** Caryophyllaceae
**Also called:** Chickweed, chickenwort, winterweed
**Uses:** Whole aboveground part, fresh or cooked
**Cautions:** Avoid during pregnancy, nursing. Possible reactions if allergic to plants in the daisy family. Look-alike species, saponins (see below).
**Season:** Spring and fall
**Range:** Throughout New Jersey and Pennsylvania; moist soil, sun to partial shade; lawns, landscaped areas, cultivated beds
**Description:** Sprawling, mat-forming. Leaves oval, pointed tip, opposite on stem. Leaf edge smooth, sometimes wavy. Fine line of hairs along the stem. Flowers at end of stem, white with 5 deeply cleft petals. Inner elastic core.

Like any plant that has "weed" in its name, common chickweed is all over the place. Chickweed is pleasantly mild, easy to harvest, and doesn't require elaborate preparation. The snipped-off tops make a tasty garnish. An open-faced sandwich topped with chickweed sprigs is exquisite.

To identify, look for the white starlike flowers. Each has five petals that are so deeply divided they look like ten. A fine line of hairs runs along the stem. When the hairs reach a pair of leaves, they flip to the other side. This is an important identifying factor.

Then there's the "rubber band" trick. Chickweed has an inner elastic core. Take a stem, bend it in half, then gently pull apart to expose the stretchy core.

Chickweed likes cool moist weather. It fades away when summer temperatures hit and returns with cooler weather. I've even harvested chickweed from under snow.

When it comes to nutrition, common chickweed compares favorably to other edible greens. It boasts significant amounts of vitamin A (in the form of beta-carotene), vitamin K, protein, iron, calcium, and magnesium.

Claims abound for chickweed's use as a cure for obesity. While the hyperbole of medical claims is rampant, there is evidence that chickweed may help in weight control. Chickweed contains saponins, flavonoids, and β-sitosterol, active compounds that may be responsible for the plant's ability to reduce appetite and decrease fat absorption. Research has shown that methanol extracts of *S. media* have anti-obesity effects, reducing body fat, at least in animal studies.

Chickweed can be added to salads, steeped for a morning cup of tea,

Five petals look like ten.

Chickweed is pretty and full of nutrition.

or added to cooked dishes. Just don't overdo it. The saponins are said to be somewhat toxic if taken in excess, but "excess" has not been defined. Saponins are much more toxic to some creatures, such as fish, than they are to humans. In large quantities, the soapy compounds may give you diarrhea or stomach upset.

A plant called scarlet pimpernel bears a resemblance to chickweed. The foliage does have a similar appearance, but scarlet pimpernel stems are square without the telltale line of hairs, and its flowers are a pinkish or coral color.

Spurge is another low-growing plant that may confuse some people. Break the stem—spurge will have a white sticky sap. If you see white sap, it may be spurge. Don't eat it.

To harvest chickweed, the stems can be broken by hand or with snippers.

There are many species worldwide. Common in our area are common chickweed (*S. media*) and mouse-ear chickweed (*Cerastium* spp.), which is hairy and considered less palatable. And then there is one very special rare species, hairy field chickweed (*Cerastium arvense* var. *villosissimum*). This native chickweed is found in Pennsylvania in the serpentine barrens of southern Lancaster and Chester Counties. The soil here has an unusual chemistry that most plants would find inhospitable, yet this chickweed thrives. It's an endangered species, so of course we won't even think about eating it.

Scarlet pimpernel is a chickweed look-alike.

When chicory is in bloom, it's hard to mistake it for any other plant.

# CHICORY
*Cichorium intybus*

**Family:** Asteraceae
**Also called:** Common chicory, succory, blue dandelion, blue daisy, blue sailors, coffee weed
**Uses:** Whole plant is edible. Flowers and young leaves raw; older leaves and roots boiled; root roasted as coffee substitute.
**Cautions:** Gas, bloating. Possible issues of allergy or with use during pregnancy.
**Season:** Leaves in spring; roots in fall; flowers summer to early fall
**Range:** Throughout New Jersey and Pennsylvania; roadsides, edges of fields, vacant lots, weedy areas
**Description:** Plant 1'–4' tall with stiff stems. Lower leaves toothed, resembling that of dandelion. Midrib is hairy on underside of leaf. Few upper leaves along stem. Flowers bright blue, rarely pink or white.

The sky-blue flowers of chicory seem almost too pretty to eat. But research confirms it as a valuable edible bursting with an assortment of nutrients. From flower to root, chicory offers a range of health benefits.

Chicory flowers can be tossed into a salad. The young leaves are eaten cooked or raw, and the taproot can be cooked like a carrot. If you've been to New Orleans, chances are you've tasted roasted chicory root mixed in with your coffee. A faux coffee can also be brewed from chicory alone for a caffeine-free beverage.

**Chicory "Coffee"**

Dig and pull chicory plants from the ground. Cut roots off and scrub to remove dirt. Cut roots into smallish pieces with a sharp knife. Spread them out on a baking sheet and roast in a 300°F oven for about 1½–2 hours, or until pieces are dry and crisp. Larger pieces will require more time. To brew: Pour 12 ounces boiling water over 2 tablespoons of roasted root chunks. Let steep for 10–15 minutes. Strain. Tasty with milk and honey.

The plant is loaded with nutrition. One cup of chopped greens (leaves) gives you one-third of your daily vitamin A requirement and more than 100 percent of your daily need for vitamin K. You also get a good helping of vitamin C, vitamin E (alpha-tocopherol), pantothenic acid, folate, manganese, and copper. In addition, chicory greens are a source of lutein and zeaxanthin, known to benefit eye health.

The roots have their own attributes. In addition to being rich in protein and minerals, chicory root contains large amounts of a substance called inulin (not to be confused with insulin). Inulin, a soluble fiber, is a powerful prebiotic that stimulates the growth of "good" bacteria in the intestines. Studies show that

Chicory flowers are fun to eat right off the plant.

inulin may also improve blood sugar control in some people with diabetes. It has even been shown to improve mood, decrease appetite, and improve memory.

Food manufacturers add inulin to many processed foods as a fat replacement and to boost fiber content. Sometimes listed as "chicory root extract," it can be found on the ingredient list of many cereals, energy bars, and healthy-type snack foods. Chicory root fiber, like other types of dietary fiber, can cause gas and digestive upset when consumed in excess.

Chicory was grown by the ancient Egyptians as a medicinal plant and a vegetable crop. It is still cultivated in Europe and many other parts of the world. Chicory greens are enjoyed in Italy, Spain, Greece, and France in a variety of dishes. Wild-foraged chicory is one of many greens used in making *horta*, a classic Greek dish. *Horta* means "weeds" in Greek. It is made from foraged indigenous plants that are boiled then dressed with olive oil and lemon juice. A traditional dish in Rome is *puntarelle*, made with chicory, anchovies, olive oil, and vinegar.

The flowers and leaves are somewhat bitter. Other bitter-flavored members of the chicory family are Belgian endive and radicchio. Adding an acid ingredient such as lemon or vinegar to the cooked greens offsets the bitterness. The addition of a fat such as olive oil also mellows the flavor, and helps absorb and transport fat-soluble vitamins.

There are no dangerous look-alike plants. The leaves can be mistaken for dandelion or wild lettuce, which are safe to eat. Chicory may trigger reactions in people who are sensitive to ragweed, daisies, or other members of the *Asteraceae* family. It may be unsafe to consume in large quantities during pregnancy; some

Chicory leaves look similar to dandelion leaves.

Chicory has long been used as food and medicine in many parts of the world.

suspect it to cause miscarriage. Although there is no medical consensus on this, stay on the safe side and avoid it.

Chicory was listed as a noxious weed in Pennsylvania until 1994, when it was officially removed from the list.

Cleavers has tiny curved hairs that make it stick to things.

## CLEAVERS
*Galium aparine*

**Family:** Rubiaceae
**Also called:** Bedstraw, catchweed, robin run the hedge, stickyweed, stickywilly, Velcro plant, clivers
**Uses:** Young growth steamed or boiled; older growth as tea; seeds as coffee substitute
**Cautions:** Sap and hairs cause skin irritation in some people. No look-alikes of concern.
**Season:** Spring
**Range:** Throughout New Jersey and Pennsylvania; along trails, edges of fields and woods, disturbed areas
**Description:** Sprawling, can grow to 6' long. Grows up and over other plants using tiny hooked hairs that enable it to cling. Square stems, easily broken. Whorls of narrow leaves at intervals along the stem. Inconspicuous tiny white flowers in small clusters in spring. Bristly fruits ⅛" across.

Cleavers is an easy plant to identify. Considered an annoying weed by most people, it has a habit of sticking to clothing and animal fur. The plant is covered with tiny backward-curving hairs. Many of its common names hint at its propensity to cling to things.

*G. aparine* is the most abundant member of its genus. Related bedstraws and cleavers can be difficult to tell apart, and none of the North American species are known to be toxic.

The name *Galium* comes from the Greek word *gala*, meaning "milk." For centuries, the plant has been used in Europe as rennet to curdle milk for yogurt and cheese. When matted together, cleavers is also employed as a sieve to strain impurities from milk.

All aboveground parts of the plant are edible. Granted, the sticky feel does not make cleavers seem very appealing as food, but there are ways to deal with the texture issue. Cooking will soften cleavers. Young leaves and stem tips can be steamed or boiled and eaten as a vegetable. Simply cook, drain, and season for a nutritious side dish. Or add chopped cleavers to your favorite soup and simmer until tender. The plant becomes more fibrous with age, so stick with young growth. Tougher plant parts can be steeped for a nutritious tea. To enjoy it in the raw state, blend the leaves and plant tips into a fruit smoothie. The seeds can be roasted and made into a good quality caffeine-free coffee substitute. Cleavers and coffee are in the same botanical family.

To harvest, no tools are needed. The stem tips break off easily. They have a pleasant scent that can be described as fresh-mown grass.

Cleavers is often used with other herbs as a spring tonic drink. Tea from the plant has a long history of medicinal use to treat skin problems such as eczema and psoriasis. It is also taken as a diuretic, and historically has been used in Europe to treat obesity. There is insufficient evidence to recommend its use as

## RECIPE

**Stickywilly Smoothie**

For one serving: Collect enough stem tips and leaves for a good handful. Rinse well, then roughly chop.

Put the following into the blender:

½ cup juice (apple or orange work well)
Handful of chopped cleavers
½ cup fresh berries, any type
½ banana

Blend until liquified. Thin with more juice if desired.

When matted together, cleavers can be used as a sieve.

medicine. The plant is rich in vitamin C. The seeds are nutritious and contain beta-carotene, lutein, and lycopene, important antioxidants.

Cleavers has some interesting non-food uses. The dried plant was once used in Europe as stuffing for mattresses, and a red dye can be made from the root.

In addition to sticking to clothing, cleavers also sticks to itself very well. If you forget to bring a strainer on your next camping trip, a makeshift version can be fashioned from a bunch of cleavers, handy when you need to drain some pasta. If you are one of the people who experiences skin irritation from cleavers, avoid using it for food or other purposes.

Curly dock leaves have wavy edges.

## CURLY DOCK
*Rumex crispus*

**Family:** Polygonaceae

**Also called:** Curled dock, yellow dock, narrowleaf dock, sour dock

**Uses:** Young leaves edible; root as medicine

**Cautions:** Oxalates, excess use

**Season:** Spring

**Range:** Throughout New Jersey and Pennsylvania; a common weed of roadsides, waste areas, fields, lawns

**Description:** Perennial. Basal rosette of leaves, each up to 12" long, lance shaped. Leaf edges are "crisped," or wavy, hence the species name. All species have a papery sheath (ocrea) at the base of each leaf petiole. Stem to 4' tall. Small, greenish flowers form reddish-brown seed clusters. Long yellow taproot.

Curly dock is another one of those vegetables that disguises itself as a weed. The plant has a worldwide history of use as food.

Dock leaves are an excellent source of vitamins, delivering more vitamin C than oranges and more vitamin A than carrots. One cup of the raw greens provides more than 100 percent of your daily requirement for those nutrients, plus high levels of protein, magnesium, iron, and other vital minerals. The greens also are rich in flavonoids, which are important in disease prevention.

Curly dock starting to put up a flower stalk; leaves may be bitter.

Gather the young leaves in early spring. Once the flower stalk forms, the leaves become impossibly bitter. Younger leaves are quite tasty. Add them to salads, or prepare as cooked greens.

## RECIPE

**White Beans and Spring Greens**

3 tablespoons extra virgin olive oil
4–5 cloves garlic, minced
4 cups chopped curly dock
4 cups mixed wild greens (dandelion, nettles, chickweed, etc.)
Pinch of red pepper flakes
2 (15-ounce) cans (4 cups cooked) cannellini beans, drained
Juice of ½ lemon
¼ cup water
¼ cup grated Parmesan cheese
Salt and pepper to taste

Heat the oil in a large skillet over medium heat. Add the garlic. Cook for 1 minute. Add the greens and red pepper flakes. Cook, stirring until the greens are wilted. Add the beans, lemon juice, and ¼ cup water. Cook until heated through. Stir in the cheese. Cook for 1–2 minutes until a creamy sauce has formed. Season with salt and pepper as desired.

The lemony taste of dock leaves comes from oxalic acid, which is known to bind with calcium. While it does keep a portion of the calcium in that food from being absorbed, this is not a concern with regards to calcium deficiency. Overall, the total nutrient content of the vegetable far outweighs concerns related to oxalic acid content. Just don't rely on dock for your calcium.

If you are at risk for kidney stones and your doctor has advised limiting spinach and other high-oxalate foods, add dock to that list. Excessive amounts may also cause stomach upset and diarrhea. High-oxalate foods tend to be very nutrient-rich, however, and most of us can safely enjoy them in normal quantities.

The root of curly dock is very bitter and generally not eaten. It has a history of use in folk medicine for many conditions, but scientific studies to support medicinal use are sparse.

In addition to its use as food, dock is used to soothe the discomfort of a stinging nettle encounter, and there is much anecdotal evidence to support this use. The leaves are crushed and applied to the affected area. Even if simply a placebo, I am a believer. I have found that both curly and broadleaf dock work.

There are many species of edible dock worldwide. Curly dock and broadleaf dock (*R. obtusifolius*) are very common. The two plants are often confused with each other. Broadleaf dock has wider leaves that are not as wavy, and usually has a reddish color to the stalk and midrib. Curly dock leaves are markedly wavy on the edges, and do not have the same reddish coloring. Curly dock is generally the less bitter of the two.

Curly dock seeds are edible and high in antioxidants.

In spring, curly dock leaves can be found in weedy, sunny habitats. The youngest leaves that are still unfurling will have a coating of mucilage and will be the most tender. Summer heat increases bitterness. If you find a plant that looks like it might be tasty even though it's late in the season, pinch off a piece of leaf and taste it. You'll know whether to harvest and bring it home. Reddish-brown dried seed stalks from the previous year may have new growth emerging at the base. Look for ruffly-edged young leaves.

Curly dock seeds are also edible. The plant is related to buckwheat, whose seeds are a nutritious food. Analysis shows that curly dock flowers and seeds are especially high in antioxidants. Dock seeds can be eaten raw or cooked. The chaff is loosened and winnowed off, and the seeds can then be used in cooked dishes or ground into flour.

Curly dock is native to Europe and western Asia and is naturalized all over the world.

Edible leaves of dame's rocket

# DAME'S ROCKET
*Hesperis matronalis*

**Family:** Brassicaceae (formerly Cruciferae)
**Also called:** Sweet rocket, dame's violet, damask violet, night-scented gillyflower, lady-of-the-evening
**Uses:** Flowers, young leaves
**Cautions:** Look-alikes
**Season:** Spring–early summer
**Range:** Throughout New Jersey and Pennsylvania; common along roadsides, edges of fields, meadows, gardens, urban woods
**Description:** Loose clusters of white, pink, or purple flowers, each with 4 petals, fragrant in the evening. Plant is 2'–3' tall. Leaves are pubescent (fuzzy) above and below, up to 6" long, usually serrated, alternately arranged on stem, becoming smaller toward top of the stem. Upper leaves sessile; lower leaves have short petioles and may be toothier. Long narrow seedpods.

Dame's rocket is such an attractive and common wildflower that many people assume it is native. If you've ever noticed tall showy purplish blooms along roadsides in late spring it is likely this plant.

Bouquet-worthy dame's rocket was introduced from Europe in the 1600s and has been making itself at home here ever since, spreading far and wide across the natural landscape. It tends to crowd out other species, and many states, including New Jersey and Pennsylvania, list dame's rocket as invasive. Although frowned upon by ecologists, it is still sold in garden centers and is often included in "wildflower" seed mixes. It's a hard plant to contain and will quickly jump the garden wall and naturalize into surrounding areas.

The young leaves of dame's rocket are eaten in many countries. Europeans enjoy them as an addition to salads, where their peppery tang accentuates milder greens. Dame's rocket shares the spicy flavor profile of other vegetables in the mustard family, which includes arugula and watercress. After the plant flowers, the leaves become stronger tasting and can be cooked in a change of water to mellow the flavor.

The flowers are milder than the leaves, although they too have a hint of mustardy zest. Enjoy them as a trail nibble, or toss them onto a simple salad for an elegant touch.

The leaves are rich in vitamin C and have historically been used to prevent or treat scurvy. The seeds are high in protein and linolenic acid, an essential fatty acid.

Dame's rocket is often confused with phlox. When I point out dame's rocket on foraging walks, I can almost guarantee someone in the group will say, "Oh, I thought that was phlox." To tell the difference just count the petals: Dame's rocket has four; phlox has five. Also, dame's rocket leaves are alternately arranged, and phlox are opposite. Not all phlox is safe to eat, so err on the side of caution

Beautiful blooms of dame's rocket

Dame's rocket flowers are sometimes white.

and don't. Dame's rocket also resembles money plant (*Lunaria annua*), a common garden plant. This one is also in the mustard family and is edible.

The genus name *Hesperis* comes from the Greek word for "evening." The plant was so named because its sweet violet-like fragrance is released at night.

Dame's rocket is a food source for butterflies and hummingbirds. Shades of purple, pink, and white flowers can be found on the same plant. After the flowers fade, long thin seedpods called siliques appear. The seeds can be sprouted and eaten.

A native of Italy, dame's rocket is now widely found in Europe, the Mediterranean region, Russia, Asia, and the United States.

## RECIPE

**Gourmet Avocado Toast**

1 avocado, pitted
2 teaspoons extra virgin olive oil
½ lemon, juiced
1 clove garlic, minced, or ½ teaspoon garlic powder
Salt and pepper to taste
Handful of dame's rocket flowers
4 slices bread, toasted

Put avocado flesh into a bowl and mash with the back of a fork. Add olive oil, lemon juice, garlic powder, and salt and pepper to taste. Mix well. Spread onto toast, open-face style. Garnish with dame's rocket flowers.

The entire dandelion plant is edible. The unopened flower buds are nice and chewy.

# DANDELION
*Taraxacum officinale*

**Family:** Asteraceae
**Also called:** Common dandelion, blowballs
**Uses:** Entire plant, raw or cooked
**Cautions:** Allergy possible
**Season:** Year-round
**Range:** Throughout New Jersey and Pennsylvania
**Description:** Leaves are basal, up to 10" long, shallow to deeply toothed. Smooth, hollow unbranched stalk, milky sap when broken. One yellow flower per stalk, bloom time is April–May. Seed head is familiar puffball. Long taproot.

The common dandelion is one of the most underappreciated edible plants. From the root to the blossom, it is a powerhouse of nutrition.

Dandelion greens are a good source of B vitamins, vitamin C, folate, magnesium, copper, vitamin E, calcium, iron, potassium, manganese, and dietary fiber. One-half cup of cooked leaves provides almost the full daily requirement for vitamin A, needed for vision, cell growth, and immunity. The leaves are exceptionally high in vitamin K, vital for blood clotting, heart health, and bone strength. If any wild plant deserves to be called a nutritional superstar, this is it.

Dandelion is commonly used by herbalists to treat a wide range of health conditions, and it has been valued as a medicinal herb for centuries by cultures around the world. There may be a scientific basis for traditional uses of the plant.

A growing body of evidence shows that dandelion possesses bioactive constituents that may have the potential to prevent or treat obesity, heart disease, diabetes, cancer, and more. Promising lab studies show dandelion root extract to be effective against human cancer cells. The extract has demonstrated effectiveness against melanoma, leukemia, pancreatic, and colon cancer cells, with no toxicity to healthy cells. Dandelion root has long been used to treat liver ailments, and modern research suggests that dandelion may promote liver health by protecting it from oxidative stress.

Dandelions are rich in antioxidant polyphenols. The flowers are especially high in these protective substances. They also contain lutein and zeaxanthin for eye health. Dandelion roots contain inulin, a prebiotic that may help to maintain a healthy digestive tract. The bitterness in the leaves is due to sesquiterpene lactones, substances that possess anti-inflammatory, antimicrobial, and other health benefits.

The word "dandelion" comes from the French for "teeth of the lion." The scientific name, *Taraxacum officinale,* translates as "official remedy."

It is often said that once the plant has bloomed, dandelion leaves become too bitter to eat. This is not always the case. Bitterness varies depending on the plant, location, season, and weather. Plants growing in shade will be milder than those growing in a sunny lawn. If the greens you've foraged are too bitter for your taste, they can be blanched. Boil for 2 or 3 minutes, drain, and rinse under cold water. Squeeze out excess water, chop, and proceed to use in any recipe that calls for greens.

Dandelions dotting a lawn

**Dandelion-Strawberry Salad**

Bowlful of spring dandelion greens, torn or chopped
A few sliced strawberries
¼ red onion, thinly sliced
2 ounces goat cheese
Simple vinaigrette, homemade or bottled

Combine the greens, strawberries, and onion. Drizzle with salad dressing and toss. Dab on the goat cheese.

Techniques for enjoying dandelion in a salad include pairing the greens with rich fatty flavors (goat cheese, salad dressing, etc.) and sweet or acid elements to balance the bitterness. The classic Pennsylvania Dutch dandelion salad with hot bacon dressing is a perfect example—the recipe usually calls for sugar and vinegar in addition to rich, fatty bacon.

Don't worry about overharvesting. When you dig up a root of this tenacious perennial, fragments are often left behind and will grow a new plant. While this may be cursed by lawn-lovers, it's good news to those of us who are happy to have a renewable year-round super vegetable available in our backyard.

The "puff" of a dandelion, ready to spread its seed to the dismay of lawn-lovers

Dandelions were originally brought to America from Europe. For centuries they were treasured for beauty, culinary use, nutrition, and medicine. In the twentieth century, perceptions changed and the dandelion became a "weed," a contaminant that marred the beauty of pure turf lawns. But they are still appreciated in many places and are grown as a commercial crop in Bulgaria, Hungary, Poland, Romania, and the United Kingdom.

There are several dandelion imposters that may have similar leaves and yellow flowers, but none are poisonous. They include hawkbit, chicory, wild lettuce, cat's ear, hawksbeard, hawkweed, shepherd's purse, and sow thistle.

Eastern white pine

## EASTERN WHITE PINE
*Pinus strobus*

**Family:** Pinaceae
**Also called:** White pine, northern white pine
**Uses:** Needles for tea; inner bark as food source
**Cautions:** Similarity to toxic species. Pine wood and resin may cause dermatitis.
**Season:** Year-round
**Range:** Throughout New Jersey and Pennsylvania; common in woodlands
**Description:** Large evergreen tree, up to 150'. Needles 3"–5" long, soft, flexible, 5 to a fascicle (bundle). Female cones 4"–7" long, hang from branches; male cones are small, yellow, less conspicuous.

Did you know that you can eat a pine tree? Our native white pine is actually a giant wild edible plant. And while you wouldn't just start gnawing on the bark like a porcupine, there are numerous ways to put pine on your menu and utilize its culinary and nutritional goodness.

There are various species of pine, not all equally edible. Here we will discuss eastern white pine, since it is readily available and easy to identify.

**White Pine Tea**

⅓ cup white pine needles
1 cup boiling water
Sweetener (optional)

Roughly chop the needles and put them into a large mug. Pour boiling water over and let steep for a few minutes. Strain. Sweeten if you prefer.

The most common way to "eat" a pine is to make tea from the needles. Fresh white pine needles can be brewed into a hot beverage that is a palatable and reliable source of vitamin C, available even in winter months. Analysis shows that winter needles have approximately double the vitamin C content of spring needles. The needles are also high in other antioxidants, including resveratrol, xanthophyll, and lutein.

The winged seeds found in the female cones are edible but are small and fiddly and hardly worth the bother. These cones have a classic pinecone appearance and hang from the upper branches. Male pinecones are tiny and found near the tips of lower branches. They can be boiled and eaten whole.

White pine needles, chopped for tea

Eastern white pine in spring

A number of Native American tribes ate the inner bark of white pine in times of food scarcity. The word "Adirondack," meaning "bark eaters," was a derogatory term used by the Mohawk Indians to describe their neighbors, the Algonquins.

My first experience chewing the inner bark of a huge fallen pine bough was surprisingly pleasant. Subsequent "tastings" from other trees have led me to understand that the flavor can really vary from tree to tree. The rubbery texture reminds me of chewing gum. This edible inner layer is located between the rough outer bark and the wood inside the tree. Stripping the bark from a living tree can kill it, so look for freshly fallen branches. With a knife, peel away the bark to expose the cream-colored inner bark. It will easily peel into strips, which can then be fried, boiled, or dried to make flour.

You may notice an amber-colored substance oozing from the bark of pine trees. This gooey stuff is pine resin, or sap; the tree secretes it to seal wounds. When still soft, you can eat bits of it straight off the tree. Pine resin is said to be soothing for sore throats.

Retsina is a Greek wine made since ancient times. Wine was stored in clay vessels coated with pine resin to make them waterproof. The wine was inadvertently infused with pine flavor, which was not always considered a desirable trait. But the resinous retsina has grown in popularity and is now a source of cultural pride. Modern Greek wine makers achieve the effect by adding pieces of pine resin to fermenting wine.

There are no poisonous parts of a white pine tree. A source of vitamin C, it can prevent scurvy and can be viewed as survival food.

White pine needles are grouped in bundles of five.

Ponderosa pine, and possibly other species, is known to be toxic to animals and may possibly be unsafe for humans. Stick with the safe and sure white pine, which has five needles per fascicle. Ponderosa pine needles are 5–10 inches long, and are usually in bundles of three, occasionally two.

The tallest tree of any type in the northeastern United States is a white pine in Cook Forest State Park, Pennsylvania, measured at 184 feet tall.

White pine was once highly prized for its use as ship masts. It was among the first American trees brought to Europe and is now considered an invasive species in central Europe.

White pine bark is eaten by beavers, porcupines, rabbits, and mice. Squirrels and many birds feed on the seeds.

Garlic mustard is invasive and weedy but quite nutritious.

# GARLIC MUSTARD
## *Alliaria petiolata*

**Family:** Brassicaceae
**Also called:** Hedge garlic, jack-by-the-hedge, sauce-alone
**Uses:** Entire plant, raw or cooked
**Cautions:** Cyanide compounds, look-alike species
**Season:** Year-round
**Range:** Throughout Pennsylvania and New Jersey; roadsides, disturbed places, shaded areas, trailsides, forest understory
**Description:** Biennial plant. Leaves simple, unlobed. First-year basal rosette has round or kidney-shaped leaves with scalloped edges. Can stay green through winter and resume growth in spring. Second year produces a flowering stalk, 2'–3' tall with pointed, heart-shaped, sharply toothed leaves, alternate on the stem. Small white, 4-petaled flowers. Seedpods are long, thin, and 4-sided with tiny black seeds. White taproot. All parts of the plant smell of garlic when crushed.

It shouldn't be hard to find this plant. Since its introduction from Europe in the 1860s, garlic mustard has quickly spread, invading woodlands throughout northeastern United States. It was likely brought by settlers, who valued it for its culinary and medicinal uses.

Garlic mustard has a long history of use as a cooked vegetable, salad green, and garlic substitute. Its name informs you of its flavor, a robust combination of garlic and mustard.

A nutritious leafy green, garlic mustard can be added to cooked dishes or pureed into a pesto. Tuck fresh leaves into a sandwich, or garnish a dish with sprigs of tiny white garlic mustard flowers. Grate the root as a horseradish substitute. A sprinkle of the dried seeds makes a zesty seasoning.

Garlic mustard is a nutrient-dense food. It is high in fiber, carotenoids, potassium, calcium, and magnesium, and is richer in protein than most commonly eaten vegetables. A small portion of the leaves (23 g, or less than 1 ounce) provides the recommended daily allowance of vitamin C. Its vitamin A content is greater than that of spinach. Manganese, iron, copper, and zinc levels are comparable to common leafy greens.

Garlic mustard and related mustard family foods (cabbage, broccoli, brussels sprouts, etc.) are a rich source of substances called glucosinolates. These sulfur-containing compounds are responsible for the bitter flavors and distinctive aroma of these vegetables. Scientific studies suggest that consumption of mustard family vegetables appears to be associated with a lower risk of some cancers.

Glucosinolates break down to form cyanide compounds, and the plant contains measurable amounts of these. That said, many vegetables we eat contain traces of cyanide, and the liver is very efficient at filtering it out. Garlic mustard produces the chemicals as protection against insects, and levels are not considered enough to harm humans. People in Europe have eaten garlic mustard for

Second year garlic mustard with flowers

Kidney-shaped leaves of young garlic mustard

hundreds of years in raw and cooked form, and many foragers see the issue as too inconsequential to even mention. Levels are lower in second-year plants. To be extra safe, soak or blanch the leaves before using, since the compounds are

RECIPE

**Garlic Mustard Yogurt Dressing**

½ cup garlic mustard leaves, washed, stems removed
¾ cup plain Greek yogurt
1 clove garlic, minced
1 tablespoon olive oil
1 tablespoon white vinegar or red wine vinegar
2 teaspoons prepared mustard
¼ teaspoon salt
Pinch of pepper

Combine all ingredients in a food processor or blender, and puree until smooth. Season with additional salt and pepper to taste. Refrigerate for at least 1 hour before serving. Will keep, refrigerated, for up to 3 days.

water-soluble. Enjoying an occasional garlic mustard dish is considered perfectly safe, as well as a healthy dietary addition.

Young and old garlic mustard plants look quite different from each other. First-year plants are low-growing, and the leaves are rounded with scalloped edges. In its second year, the plant goes vertical, the leaves become sharply toothed with pointed tips, and flowers appear.

First-year garlic mustard is sometimes mistaken for violet leaves, which are also fine to eat. Creeping Charlie, or ground ivy (*Glechoma hederacea*), is another look-alike, but it creeps along the ground on runners. It is also safe to eat.

Taller second-year garlic mustard might be mistaken for white snakeroot (*Ageratina altissima*). This plant is toxic. It has leaves that are opposite, across from each other on the stem. Garlic mustard stem leaves are alternate, and of course will smell garlicky when crushed. So give it the sniff test.

Garlic mustard lacks natural enemies in this part of the world, which would keep its growth in check. So harvest as much as you want. It pulls easily from the ground.

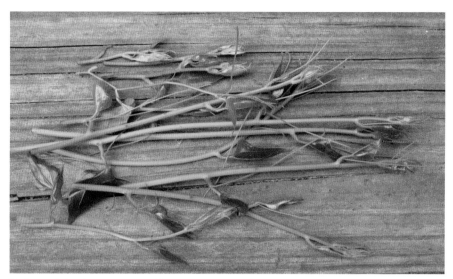

Cook greenbrier shoots as you would asparagus or green beans.

# GREENBRIER
*Smilax rotundifolia*

**Family:** Smilacaceae
**Also called:** Common greenbrier, roundleaf greenbrier, bullbrier, catbrier, horsebrier, smilax, blaspheme vine
**Uses:** Young shoots, berries, starchy roots
**Cautions:** Thorns
**Season:** Young shoots in spring; berries in fall; roots year-round
**Range:** Throughout New Jersey and Pennsylvania; along streams, edges of fields, woods, trailsides; full sun to dappled shade
**Description:** Green vine forms dense thorny thickets. Rounded heart-shaped, leathery leaves are lustrous, alternate, 2"–4" long. Leaves have parallel veins; leaf edge is smooth. Stems are solid green, may be round or angled; when mature are armed with sharp thorns. Can grow to 30' long. Climbs via soft green tendrils, which grasp and climb other plants then harden off. Inconspicuous tiny flowers in spring. Berries in late summer, dark blue-black, may be covered with powdery bloom; often persist through winter.

Thorny encounters are how most people remember this plant. Common greenbrier is usually viewed as an obnoxious vine thanks to its stout thorns that can easily tear into pants or legs. The common name blaspheme vine is no surprise, given that folks are inclined to use bad words when they find themselves entangled in it.

For positive ID, look for tendrils and thorns.

Greenbrier has awfully sharp thorns, but the springtime growth—all the tender new growing parts—are edible, and deliciously so. These young shoots include the stem, tendrils, immature leaves, and thorns. I get a kick out of eating soft thorns that haven't hardened yet.

Tender edible growth can be found mid-spring into early summer. Any part tender enough to easily snap off can be eaten. Enjoy raw as a trail nibble, or take

RECIPE

**Sautéed Smilax**

Handful of tender greenbrier tips
1 clove garlic or a few bulbs of wild garlic, chopped
Olive oil or butter
Salt and pepper to taste

Cut greenbrier into lengths of about 2 inches. Grease a skillet with 1 tablespoon or so of oil or butter. Put the garlic and greenbrier into the hot oil and cook for 2–3 minutes, stirring occasionally, until tender. Season to taste with salt and pepper.

The spring shoot is said to look like a walking stick bug.

a bunch home and cook like asparagus or green beans. Common greenbrier makes a delicious vegetable. The taste is faintly sour.

The plant has no poisonous parts. The berries are without much flavor when eaten raw, but they can be used to make jam or jelly. They will often persist on the vine throughout winter. Greenbrier roots are a source of carbohydrate calories. They are rather labor-intensive to use as a food source, although Native American tribes foraged the root starch to make bread and soup. Thinner roots are good when boiled and eaten if they are not too fibrous. Larger roots—and they can grow quite large—cannot simply be cooked like a carrot, as they are too woody. But the starch can be separated out and used as flour. To safely harvest, trace the vine down so you don't accidently harvest another plant's root. Cut up the root and crush it in water. The starch will sink to the bottom and can be collected and dried. Even though common greenbrier really is common, remember that harvesting the root will kill the plant.

There are more than 300 species of *Smilax* worldwide, with varying degrees of edibility. Many cultures have used greenbrier for a variety of medicinal reasons. The roots of some species are scientifically shown to have antioxidant and anti-inflammatory properties. Tropical *Smilax* species have been used to make the soft drink sarsaparilla.

Greenbrier is often found growing in a messy tangle with other shrubs and vines. To positively identify, make sure the vine has thorns and tendrils.

*Smilax* species are the only vines in North America that have both thorns and tendrils.

More than once I have heard someone remark that the young spring shoot looks like a walking stick bug or a praying mantis, and it does!

The thorny thickets of greenbrier provide food and refuge for many birds and small animals.

Basal rosette of leaves

## HAIRY BITTERCRESS
*Cardamine hirsuta*

**Family:** Brassicaceae or Cruciferae
**Also called:** Land cress, lamb's cress, flick weed, shotweed, common bittercress
**Uses:** All aboveground parts, raw or cooked
**Cautions:** All related look-alikes are safe to eat.
**Season:** Spring, fall
**Range:** Throughout New Jersey and Pennsylvania; moist rich soil, waste places, thin lawns; shade or sun
**Description:** Dense basal rosette of leaves radiating out from a central point. Each stem is a leaf with multiple leaflets arranged in opposite pairs. Leaflets are small and rounded; the terminal leaflet is the largest. Leaves are sparsely hairy. Flower stalk arises from the center of the rosette bearing small clusters of tiny white, 4-petaled flowers that become thin, erect seedpods. When mature, the pods explode at the lightest touch, sending seeds up to 6' away.

What an unfortunate name for a great little plant. Hairy bittercress needs a PR makeover. It's not bitter, and it's not hairy. Well, there are some minute hairs on the leaves, but you'll have to look pretty hard to find them.

**Wild Stracciatella**

3 eggs
⅓ cup finely grated Parmesan cheese
6 cups broth (chicken or vegetable)
Juice from ½ lemon
2 cups bittercress, chopped
1 cup other greens*, finely chopped
Salt and pepper to taste

Whisk eggs and ⅓ cup Parmesan together; set aside. In a large saucepan over medium heat, combine the broth and lemon juice. Bring to a boil; turn down the heat and gently simmer. Stir the broth and create a "whirlpool." Add the beaten eggs in a slow stream, stirring to break up into strands, about 1 minute. Stir in all the greens, and simmer for a few minutes until tender. Add salt and pepper if desired.

*Dandelion, violet leaves, curled dock, and garlic mustard all work.

Hairy bittercress is my favorite early green. When I see it popping up in late winter and early spring it feels like nature's signal that a new foraging cycle has begun. With its pleasant flavor and impressive nutrient profile, bittercress is a choice wild edible. *C. hirsuta* has a high antioxidant content. It's a good source of

From a compact plant to a tall lanky weed

Bittercress just starting to flower. Use as wild microgreens.

lutein, important for human eyesight, and rich in potassium, iron, and vitamin C. Calcium, magnesium, manganese, and zinc levels are comparable to conventional vegetables.

Bittercress is a member of the mustard family, also known as the cruciferous vegetables. This clan includes such famously healthy foods as kale and broccoli, all uniquely rich in glucosinolates, compounds that are responsible for their characteristic flavor (bitter or peppery) and smell (think cooked cabbage). Glucosinolates break down into compounds that are shown to have anticancer, antibacterial, and antiviral effects.

The best time to harvest bittercress is before it flowers. Find it in moist spots in vegetable beds and flower beds. It often pops up in mulched areas. When still a cute compact rosette, the plant can easily be turned into salad. It pulls up easily. Trim off the root, bring it inside, and rinse it off.

When the flower stalks appear, this little gem morphs into a taller, weedy plant. Each flower becomes an exploding seedpod.

Bittercress has a somewhat peppery flavor, like a mild version of watercress. Use the delicate leaves in salads or as a sandwich garnish to add a dose of flavor and nutrients. Hairy bittercress is an edible weed par excellence.

Hairy bittercress is native to Europe and Asia. It can be mistaken for similar members of the mustard family, but they are all considered edible, so the look-alikes are not problematic.

Don't be afraid of harvesting too much of this plant. It is very prolific and seen by many as a nuisance weed.

Henbit has a long history of food use.

## HENBIT
*Lamium amplexicaule*

**Family:** Lamiaceae
**Also called:** Henbit deadnettle, greater henbit, common henbit, giraffe head
**Uses:** Stems, flowers, and leaves; raw in salads or cooked as greens
**Cautions:** Some look-alike plants, but none are toxic.
**Season:** Late winter, spring
**Range:** Throughout New Jersey and Pennsylvania; a weed of gardens, lawns, fields, roadsides, and other disturbed areas
**Description:** Leaves rounded with scalloped edges, in opposite pairs at intervals along the stem. Upper leaves sessile and encircle the stem, lower leaves with long petioles. Stems up to 18", green or reddish; square, as typical of the mint family. Flowers ½"–¾" long, pinkish purple and tubular. The plant is finely hairy.

There is one characteristic that allows me to instantly recognize henbit—the ruffle of scalloped leaves that encircle the square stem at intervals along its length. When I see this pattern—a ruffly set of leaves, a length of stem, another set of leaves—I know I've found henbit. Pretty purplish flowers arising from the upper leaf axils are another clue.

The species name "amplexicaule" means "clasping" and refers to how henbit leaves attach to the stem directly, lacking a stalk.

Henbit is a mild-tasting green. Although it's in the mint family, it lacks a minty scent. The mild-tasting leaves, flowers, and small stems can be used in wrap sandwiches, green smoothies, or as a salad ingredient. Henbit also works well in cooked dishes like soups and casseroles and is nice brewed into a tea. It is eaten by various cultures around the world and has held a special position in Japanese cuisine since ancient times. January 7 is the day

Scalloped leaves of henbit

of the Seven Herb Festival. On this day, many Japanese people eat a traditional rice porridge called "seven spring herbs." It contains seven wild greens found in spring. While the plants used may differ from region to region, henbit is usually a requisite ingredient. The custom goes back at least 1,000 years. Eating wild greens in the New Year is believed to promote good health for the coming year. It is certainly a way to get vitamins and minerals in winter, when fresh produce can be scarce.

## RECIPE

**Henbit Green Sauce**

2 cups henbit leaves, flowers, and stems
2 cups chopped chickweed and/or deadnettle tops
3 garlic cloves, coarsely chopped
½ cup extra virgin olive oil
¼ cup grated Parmesan cheese
1 tablespoon lemon juice
Salt and pepper to taste

Put all ingredients in a food processor or blender; process until smooth. Adjust seasonings as desired. Serve over hot pasta, vegetables, etc.

Henbit on the left, deadnettle on the right

Henbit and other *Lamium* species have been shown to possess high antioxidant activity. Scientific nutrient analysis of henbit is sparse, but we do know that leafy greens as a whole are very nutritious, especially the wild varieties. So it's probably the case that henbit is one of our nourishing wild greens.

There are no poisonous look-alikes. Henbit is often confused with purple deadnettle (*L. purpureum*), and vice versa. Luckily, both are completely safe and edible. The upper leaves of deadnettle have petioles, unlike henbit.

*Glechoma hederacea*, known as ground ivy or creeping Charlie, is sometimes mistaken for henbit. Ground ivy leaves, however, have petioles and are hairless, and the plant creeps along the ground. Ground ivy is also edible.

Because henbit blooms so early it is an important early pollen and nectar source for pollinators. The flowers are attractive to long-tongued bees such as bumblebees and solitary bees, which have tongues long enough to access the nectar deep inside the long, tubular flowers. Hummingbirds and butterflies also feed on the flowers. Chickens are said to be especially fond of the plant, hence the common name.

Henbit is native to Europe, western Asia, and Africa and is widely naturalized throughout North America and other parts of the world.

Very young Japanese knotweed shoot

## JAPANESE KNOTWEED
*Polygonum cuspidatum (Fallopia japonica, Reynoutria japonica)*

**Family:** Polygonaceae

**Also called:** Knotweed, Japanese bamboo, Mexican bamboo, Himalayan fleece vine, monkeyweed, donkey rhubarb

**Uses:** Young shoots, raw or cooked

**Cautions:** Oxalic acid. No poisonous look-alikes.

**Season:** Spring

**Range:** Throughout New Jersey and Pennsylvania; along forest edges, streams, rivers, roadsides, disturbed areas

**Description:** Perennial herbaceous plant, can grow 10' or taller in one season. Stems are green or reddish, smooth, hollow, and jointed, resembling bamboo. Leaves are simple, entire, spade-shaped, arranged in a zigzag pattern. Delicate whitish flower clusters grow from leaf nodes in late summer.

Japanese knotweed was introduced into the United States from Asia in the late 1800s as a garden ornamental and for erosion control. The exotic bamboo-like plant is quite pretty, especially when flowering, but it spreads aggressively and creates monocultures that crowd out other plants. Its powerful roots are able to break through pavement and building foundations. Japanese knotweed has earned a reputation as one of the worst invasive species in the country.

So forage this one with abandon. In spring the plant pushes up new growth. The succulent young shoots are tart and nutritious. They resemble short, stout asparagus stems. Harvest before they reach 8 inches tall and are still tender. When small they can easily be snapped, and no cutting tools are needed. As the plant matures, it turns fibrous and inedible.

Japanese knotweed works well in both sweet and savory dishes. When preparing the shoots, the leaves are usually removed. Smaller curled leaves at the top—they look like arrowheads—are palatable enough to be eaten. Stalks won't need to be peeled unless the skin seems tough.

Knotweed can be enjoyed raw, as in a tart version of celery. The stems are hollow. This feature lends itself nicely to stuffing; think cream cheese, peanut butter, or hummus. It can be cooked or baked into desserts. Use it in any recipe that calls for rhubarb; the taste is similar. It is often made into jam and pickles. Knotweed shoots can be steamed and served with butter or a sauce. Slice and add to soups to lend a sour note.

These older stems may need to be peeled.

In Asia knotweed is known as *itadori*, and the spring shoots are a popular "mountain vegetable," or foraged plant. The root is used to make *itadori* tea, a traditional remedy for preventing heart disease and strokes.

Lab research has provided evidence that Japanese knotweed has anti-inflammatory and anticancer properties. It has displayed strong activity against the bacteria that cause Lyme disease. Japanese knotweed is an exceptional source of resveratrol, the same healthful antioxidant found in grapes and red wine. It has one of the highest concentrations of resveratrol found in the plant world. The highest concentration is in the root, which is not usually eaten. Supplement manufacturers extract resveratrol from Japanese knotweed roots and market it for a variety of conditions, including Lyme disease. Although such supplements may not be approved by the FDA, studies show that resveratrol appears quite safe.

The best time to get to know this plant is in summer, when it is easily recognizable. The tall stalks will be woody, but you'll know where to come back to in spring. The young shoots will be sprouting among the old dry stalks.

When foraging Japanese knotweed, keep in mind that this invasive is a common target for eradication and may have been treated with herbicides. Sometimes chemicals are injected into the stems. The plants may still look healthy for a while, so exercise caution. Ask the landowner, if possible. Many people would be pleased to have someone remove Japanese knotweed from their property.

## RECIPE

**Strawberry Knotweed Fruit Crisp**

3 cups sliced Japanese knotweed shoots, leaves removed
2 cups sliced fresh strawberries
⅓ cup sugar
½ cup old-fashioned oats
¼ cup flour
½ cup brown sugar, lightly packed
½ teaspoon cinnamon
½ stick (2 ounces) butter

Preheat oven to 350°F. In a bowl, mix knotweed, strawberries, and sugar. Place in a lightly greased 2-quart baking dish. Combine the oats, flour, brown sugar, and cinnamon. Cut in the butter (use a pastry blender, or quickly break up with fingers) until mixture resembles coarse meal. Sprinkle over the fruit filling. Bake for 30–35 minutes, or until golden on top. Serve warm or at room temperature.

Stems are sliced and ready for cooking.

Like a number of other nutritious vegetables, including spinach, Japanese knotweed contains oxalic acid. Avoid this vegetable if your medical provider has advised you to limit your oxalic acid intake.

Maple sap drips from a spile.

## MAPLE
*Acer* spp.

**Family:** Sapindaceae
**Also called:** Sugar maple (hard maple, rock maple), red maple (swamp maple, soft maple)
**Uses:** Sap, seeds, young leaves
**Cautions:** None
**Season:** Sap in late winter / early spring, leaves in spring, seeds in spring / summer
**Range:** Throughout New Jersey and Pennsylvania
**Description:** Deciduous tree with opposite branching. Leaves opposite, palmately lobed. Fruit is a double samara.

Maple syrup is made from the boiled down sap of a maple tree. But the tree offers more than just a sweet confection to pour on pancakes.

As it exits the tree, maple sap looks like clear water. It can be consumed as is and provides a safe freshwater source. After the sap is made into syrup, it can be boiled down further into maple sugar. The seeds can be eaten raw as a trail nibble or cooked in a variety of ways. Even young maple leaves are edible.

The sugar maple has the highest concentration of sugar.

There are more than one hundred species of maple worldwide. Red maple, sugar maple, and silver maple are the most common native maples in our area. Introduced species include Norway and Japanese maples. All maples have basically the same edible properties.

Maple trees can be tapped for sap when the days are warm and the nights are freezing. This involves drilling a small hole in the trunk, inserting a spile, and collecting the dripping sap.

Boiling the sap concentrates the sugar. It is often said that it takes 40 gallons of sap to produce 1 gallon of syrup. But the yield depends on the sugar content of your sap: Your mileage may vary depending on the sap, the tree, weather, and the location. Sugar content ranges from 1 to 5 percent. The sap of the sugar maple (*A. saccharum*) has the highest concentration.

European settlers learned how to create maple syrup from the native people, who discovered the technique. Native Americans made cuts into tree trunks and collected sap with spiles made of hollowed-out stems. The sap was boiled in a hollowed wood vessel by dropping hot rocks into it, since they did not have metal pots. An alternate way to concentrate sap was to allow it to freeze, discarding the ice layer that formed.

Sugar maple leaf

**Curried Samaras**

Maple seeds
Melted butter
Salt and curry powder to taste

Collect plump green maple seeds, and soak them in water for about 1 hour. (This makes it easier to remove the wings and skins.) Remove seeds, and spread them out on a baking sheet. Bake at 350°F for 8–10 minutes, or until crisp. Drizzle with melted butter, add salt, and sprinkle with curry powder.

Maple syrup contains vitamins, amino acids, antioxidants, and minerals such as iron, calcium, zinc, and manganese. The level of manganese is especially high. Two tablespoons of syrup provide 1.3 mg, or two-thirds of the required daily value for adults. Manganese is a component of superoxide dismutase (SOD), which has been called the most important antioxidant in the body, essential in preventing cellular damage. The syrup also contains inulin (not to be confused with insulin), a substance that contributes to colon heath by promoting the growth of beneficial bacteria.

A 10-foot-tall maple samara

Darker syrup, classified as Grade B, is made from sap obtained later in the season. It has a more pronounced flavor and higher levels of antioxidants than lighter syrup. Maple syrup has more antioxidants than refined sugar. But while maple syrup may be more healthful than some other sugars, it does not give us a free pass to consume in copious quantity. It's still mostly sugar. Enjoy it as an occasional treat.

To positively identify your tree as a maple, look at the leaf. It should look similar to the stylized red maple leaf on the Canadian flag. The branches should be situated opposite each other. The seeds of maples are winged samaras that come in fused pairs. Samaras twirl to the ground when they fall, hence the nicknames helicopters and whirligigs. In my childhood they were called pollynoses. You would find a green one, split it at the seed end, and stick it on your nose to make a green parrot nose.

When the fiddleheads unfurl, the fronds become toxic.

## OSTRICH FERN
*Matteuccia struthiopteris*

**Family:** Onocleaceae
**Also called:** Shuttlecock fern, fiddlehead fern
**Uses:** Young unfurled leaf, cooked
**Cautions:** Must be cooked
**Season:** Spring
**Range:** New Jersey and Pennsylvania; in swamps, wetlands, along creeks, under the shade of canopy trees; shade to part sun
**Description:** A perennial plant with 2 leaf types. Sterile fronds are showy, green, finely dissected, 2'–6' tall, resembling ostrich plumes. They are wider from middle to tip, forming a vase-shaped clump. A deep, U-shaped groove runs the length of the smooth green stem. The leaf, tightly coiled when young, is known as a fiddlehead. It is covered with brownish papery scales that fall away as the coil unfolds. The fertile fronds arise in midsummer. They are shorter, brown, and also have a groove on the inner side of the stem. No flowers.

Fiddleheads, so called because the tightly furled tops look like the head of a fiddle, are a delicious springtime vegetable. They were an important food of the native people of eastern North America, who introduced them to early settlers.

The young coiled fiddlehead is the only part of the ostrich fern that can be eaten. As it unrolls to become the plumelike frond, it becomes toxic.

**Sautéed Fiddleheads with Butter and Lemon**

1 cup ostrich fern fiddleheads
1 tablespoon butter
Lemon juice, salt, pepper to taste

Rinse the fiddleheads well in cold water, removing all brown papery bits. Trim stems if longer than 2 inches. Bring a pot of water to a boil. Add the fiddleheads to the boiling water and cook for 10 minutes. Drain. Melt butter in a skillet over medium heat. Add the drained fiddleheads. Sauté, stirring occasionally, until lightly browned, about 5–7 minutes. Remove from heat and season as desired with salt, pepper, and a splash of lemon.

Nearly all ferns produce a fiddlehead, but not all fiddleheads are equally edible. Several species have historically been used as food. The ostrich fern is the most commonly harvested in the northeastern United States.

Bracken fern (*Pteridium aquilinum*) is found throughout the world and eaten in many countries. There is a great deal of controversy about whether it should be consumed at all, as it is a suspected human carcinogen. To avoid problematic species, we will stick with the ostrich fern. To identify, look for the brown papery

Note the papery scales and U-shaped groove on the stem.

New and old fronds of ostrich fern

scale-like covering on the coiled fern, and a smooth stem (not fuzzy) with a deep U-shaped groove on the inner side.

The brown fertile fronds can persist through winter, indicating where new growth may be found in spring. Ostrich fern fiddleheads arise in a clump, known as a "crown," which may be covered in moss or leaf debris. Each fiddlehead is only about 1 inch in diameter. A mature plant may have six to eight or more per crown. Pick no more than one-half from any given crown, as overharvesting may kill the plant. Choose only tightly coiled specimens. Fiddleheads can be easily snapped off, or they can be cut with a knife. The stem can be eaten as well, as long as the top is still tightly furled. Fresh fiddleheads can be refrigerated for five to seven days.

Although numerous books and online sources describe eating fiddleheads raw, this is not advised. Resist the temptation to nibble in the field. Fiddleheads should not be eaten raw or undercooked. In the 1990s several outbreaks of food poisoning occurred in New York and western Canada associated with inadequately cooked ostrich fern fiddleheads. Nausea, vomiting, headache, abdominal cramps, and diarrhea were the most commonly reported symptoms. Researchers linked the illness to fiddleheads that were eaten raw, sautéed, parboiled, or microwaved.

Tightly coiled fiddleheads of ostrich fern

Thorough cooking is necessary to eliminate the toxin. The Centers for Disease Control (CDC) recommends boiling fiddleheads for 10 minutes before eating. Discard the cooking water. The cooked fiddleheads can then be served or used as an ingredient in other dishes.

Ostrich fern fiddleheads have an impressive nutrient composition. Analysis has shown an unusual amount and combination of fatty acids, including omega-3 eicosapentaenoic acid (EPA), which is not usually found in plants but rather in fatty cold-water fish. The fiddleheads were found to have the most complete fatty acid profile of any edible green plant. Extraordinarily high levels of antioxidant activity were measured for ostrich fern. It is a rich source of carotene, violaxanthin, zeaxanthin, lutein, gallic acid, and vitamins C and E.

Native plantain, *P. rugelii*

## PLANTAIN
### *Plantago* spp.

**Family:** Plantaginaceae
**Also called:** Common plantain, blackseed plantain, broadleaf plantain, ribwort, English plantain, narrowleaf plantain, buckhorn
**Uses:** Leaves and seeds, raw or cooked
**Cautions:** None; no problematic look-alikes
**Season:** Spring, summer
**Range:** Throughout New Jersey and Pennsylvania; lawns, fields, compacted ground, waste areas
**Description:** A low-to-the-ground basal rosette. Leaves are oval, or long and narrow, depending on species. Parallel veins run from stem to leaf tip. Leaf edges are untoothed. Flowers are tiny, tan-green, clustered on a tall leafless stalk.

Plantain is a very common weed. You're almost certain to find it growing in your yard, or in any lawn that has not been tainted by herbicides. Plantain thrives in compacted soil, so it often pops up in areas of heavy foot traffic.

There are more than 200 species of *Plantago*. The green plants share a common name with the plantain banana, but they are not at all related. Three species are common in our area: common plantain (*P. major*), Rugel's plantain (*P. rugelii*), and narrowleaf plantain (*P. lanceolata*). The first two are similar and can be difficult to tell apart. The native Rugel's plantain appears to be more prevalent in this area. It has a dark red or purple petiole. Common plantain usually lacks this coloration, although it may be present.

Common plantain was introduced from Europe. Native Americans called it "white man's foot" because it seemed to appear wherever the Europeans stepped. Narrowleaf plantain can be distinguished by its long narrow leaves and

Narrowleaf plantain, also called English plantain

a seed cluster that sits at the top of the stem. Foragers use all three plantains interchangeably.

Plantain is mild tasting. Young leaves are good in salad. Tougher leaves can be chopped and cooked as a green vegetable or added to soups. Immature seed heads can be nibbled raw or boiled and buttered. Gather seeds at any stage to add fiber and protein to recipes. New tender leaves can be found on mature plants in summer.

Plantain seeds are high in fiber. Psyllium (marketed as Metamucil) is a soluble dietary fiber obtained from the seeds of several *Plantago* species.

For a mug of plantain tea, chop a few leaves (can include seed stalks), cover with boiling water, and let steep for 10 minutes. Strain, and sweeten as desired. Research shows that tea made from leaves of common plantain has effective analgesic and anti-inflammatory activities.

Common plantain is rich in calcium and other minerals, carotenoids, B vitamins, vitamin K, and vitamin C. Plantain has been valued worldwide for a range of medicinal applications. It was used by Native Americans for snakebite, infections, skin ailments, and more. Use of plantain in Chinese traditional medicine dates back to ancient times.

Plantain seeds are rich in fiber.

Plantain has been valued as food and medicine for centuries.

Plantain is a common ingredient in herbal healing salves. The crushed leaves are used to soothe stings and bug bites and to draw out splinters. A common folk remedy is the "spit poultice," in which plantain leaves are chewed and applied to an affected area.

Modern science supports many of the purported benefits. *Plantago* has astringent, demulcent, and emollient qualities, and flavonoid antioxidants that prevent cell damage. Extracts demonstrate anti-inflammatory, antimicrobial, analgesic, and wound-healing properties.

Plantain is common, so don't worry about overharvesting. To forage the leaves, simply break them off with your fingers or a pair of snippers.

Purple deadnettle in late winter

## PURPLE DEADNETTLE
*Lamium purpureum*

**Family:** Lamiaceae
**Also called:** Red deadnettle, purple archangel
**Uses:** Leaves and flowering tops, raw or cooked
**Cautions:** Look-alikes not toxic
**Season:** Late winter into spring
**Range:** Throughout New Jersey and Pennsylvania; a weed of gardens, fields, edge habitats, disturbed areas
**Description:** Herbaceous winter annual. Unbranched, up to 18" tall; stem is square. Leaves roughly heart shaped, bluntly toothed, pubescent, arranged in opposite pairs. Upper leaves take on a purplish hue once there is enough sunlight and warmth. Flowers small, tubular, bilaterally symmetrical, pink-purple.

Purple deadnettle is another of those underrated wild plants considered by most people to be a weed. One of the first edibles to emerge in late winter and early spring, it heralds the new foraging season.

Field covered in purple deadnettle

Deadnettle's scientific name, *Lamium purpureum,* translates as "the devouring purple monster." "Devouring monster" (from the Greek, *lamia*) may refer to either the appearance of the flower (open jaw) or the plant's aggressive nature. I have seen farm fields absolutely covered with purple deadnettle. The "nettle" in the name refers to the plant having a superficial resemblance to stinging nettle but without the ability to sting, hence "dead." The two plants are unrelated.

All tender parts of deadnettle are good to eat.

**Wild-Foraged Mess o' Greens**

2 cups water
2 cups deadnettle tops, chopped
4 cups assorted greens (lamb's-quarter, henbit, chickweed, violet leaves, dandelion leaves), chopped
Juice of 1 lemon
Few tablespoons extra virgin olive oil
½ teaspoon garlic powder
½ teaspoon ground cumin
Salt and pepper to taste

Add the water to a large pot; bring to a boil. Add all the greens and cook until tender. Drain the water from the greens and return greens to the pot. Add the lemon juice, a few tablespoons of olive oil, garlic, and cumin. Toss to combine. Taste; season with salt and pepper as desired.

Although it's in the mint family, deadnettle lacks a minty scent. In fact, some find the smell objectionable, but I don't pick up on that. Its flavor can be described as grassy or mildly green, never bitter. To harvest, pluck the heads of deadnettle. The leaves, flowers, and tender stems are a versatile ingredient.

Chop and add to any cooked dish where a mild green is appropriate. Use deadnettle to concoct a wild pesto or enrich a soup. Deadnettle is fine in a salad, but its fuzzy texture can be a bit off-putting. This is easily resolved by cooking, or by blending the harvested parts into a smoothie.

There are some look-alike plants, but they are edible as well. Henbit (*L. amplexicaule*) is probably the one most often confused with deadnettle. Henbit leaves, however, are scalloped. Ground ivy (*Glechoma hederacea*) also somewhat resembles deadnettle, but it creeps along the ground.

Research shows that purple deadnettle exhibits antioxidant activity and is a rich source of protein, carotene, and vitamin C. The leaves have traditionally been used as a diuretic, an expectorant, and a styptic to stop bleeding.

Deadnettle is a favorite of bees. It is an early source of pollen and nectar at a time when few other plants are in flower.

Purple deadnettle is native to Europe and Asia, and widely naturalized throughout North America. It's a nutritious and lovely springtime plant that you

Two underappreciated plants: deadnettle and dandelion

very likely have growing in your backyard or local environment, readily available to add some green nourishment to your diet.

Ramps making their brief springtime appearance

## RAMPS
*Allium tricoccum*

**Family:** Alliaceae
**Also called:** Wild leek, wood leek
**Uses:** Leaves, raw or cooked. Entire plant is edible, but harvesting the root kills the plant.
**Cautions:** Look-alike species
**Season:** Early spring
**Range:** Throughout New Jersey and Pennsylvania; moist deciduous woods; semi-shade
**Description:** Bulbous perennial with 2 or 3 broad, smooth leaves per plant. Leaf stalk and bulb are similar to a scallion, lower stalk white or reddish. As the leaves wither, the flower stalk appears. Flowers are white in a terminal umbel. Round, shiny black seeds ripen in fall.

Wild ramps are a spring ephemeral and one of the first plants to appear in eastern woodlands. A member of the onion family, ramps are our native wild leek. They were an important vegetable food of Native American people. Cherokee tribes and European settlers utilized the plant to treat colds and other maladies and foraged it as a spring tonic. To this day, residents of the Appalachian region of the United States gather the pungently aromatic plant as a rite of spring.

Historically, ramps served to replenish nutrients lacking in a winter diet of stored foods like dried beans and meat. Rich in vitamin C, ramps were a key ingredient in preventing scurvy. The bulbs contain sulfur compounds, including allicin, that are antioxidant and antibacterial. Ramps also contain selenium, a

**Ramp Butter**

8–10 ramp leaves, finely minced
2 sticks butter, softened at room temperature
1 tablespoon lemon juice
⅛ teaspoon pepper
Salt to taste

Combine all ingredients in a medium bowl. Scoop onto a piece of plastic wrap, and roll into a log shape. Twist the ends to seal. Chill until firm. To use: Slice and add to hot vegetables, baked potato, toast, pasta, etc. Ramp butter keeps for 2 weeks refrigerated, or up to 12 months in the freezer. Savor the flavor of ramps all year long!

mineral that may boost immunity and lower cancer risk and cognitive decline. Science appears to validate some of the traditional medicinal uses of ramps.

A colony of wild ramps

Ramp leaves are very tasty.

Ramps are popularly fried with potatoes in bacon grease, cooked with scrambled eggs, added to salads, and pickled. Ramp flowers are eaten and used as a garnish.

Throughout the Appalachian states, ramp festivals are held each spring to celebrate the annual return of the cherished vegetable. In the 1990s, ramps surged onto the culinary scene and became a gourmet food item across the country. High-end restaurants competed to have ramps on their menu. Demand exceeded supply, as foragers overharvested plants to sell them to restaurants and farm markets. Many wild ramp colonies were decimated. They are now in decline in some areas from the Appalachian Mountains up to Quebec. Ramps reproduce slowly, taking five to seven years to reach maturity.

It is generally agreed that there is a need to protect ramp populations. Instead of the usual practice of digging up whole plants, most foragers who promote sustainable harvesting now take only leaves, or remove just one leaf per plant, leaving the bulb in the ground. Some foragers still uproot the whole plant but advise taking only a small percentage of the total patch.

The native Cherokee people in North Carolina have harvested ramps for more than 10,000 years using practices passed down over the centuries that appear to have had little negative impact on ramp colonies. Their method consists of cutting the stem and leaves above the bulb, never pulling the bulb or root

Ramps on the left; lily of the valley on the right

from the ground, and taking not more than 10 percent of any given patch at a time.

A poisonous lookalike to be aware of is lily of the valley (*Convallaria majalis*). To be certain you have a ramp, crush a leaf. It should have a distinct garlic or onion odor. Lily of the valley lacks this odor and does not have a bulb.

Ramps are pollinated by bees and other insects, and mammals (other than humans) rarely feed on the plant.

Cauliflorous flowers blooming directly from the main trunk

## REDBUD
*Cercis canadensis*

**Family:** Fabaceae / Leguminosae
**Also called:** Judas tree, eastern redbud
**Uses:** Flowers and flower buds eaten raw, added to salad; buds pickled as a caper substitute; tender young pods sautéed
**Cautions:** No look-alikes
**Season:** Spring
**Range:** Throughout New Jersey and Pennsylvania; understory tree; can tolerate sunny forest edges
**Description:** Small deciduous tree, growing to 20'–30'. Leaves are alternate, simple, heart shaped, 3"–5" long with smooth margins. The fruit is a flat pod, 2"–3" long, that often persists on the tree through winter. Rosy pink flowers are cauliflorous, growing directly on major branches and trunks. The flowers are very showy, covering the tree in early spring before leaves appear. They have a pealike shape.

Our native eastern redbud is one of the first trees to bloom in spring. It's also one of the showiest, boasting magenta flowers that adorn bare branches before the first leaves emerge.

Redbud is a feast for the taste buds as well as the eyes. The flowers have a pleasant, slightly tart flavor. They are nice eaten raw and can be added to baked goods or made into jellies. Tossed into a salad, they add a definite wow factor.

RECIPE

**Redbud Muffins**

**Yield:** 12

2 cups flour

½ cup sugar

1 tablespoon baking powder

½ teaspoon salt

2 cups redbud blossoms

2 large eggs

1 cup milk

¼ cup vegetable oil

Preheat oven to 400°F. Lightly grease a muffin pan or use paper liners. In a large bowl, mix the flour, sugar, baking powder, and salt. In another bowl, beat the eggs, milk, and oil. Add the liquid to the dry ingredients. Combine, but don't overbeat. Fold in the redbud blossoms. Fill muffin cups about three-quarters full. Bake 15–18 minutes, or until a toothpick inserted comes out clean. Cool on a wire rack.

After their fleeting spring performance, the flowers give way to green seedpods. While still young and tender, the pods can be prepared like snow peas, which they resemble. They're suitable in a stir-fry, or simply steamed and seasoned. Native Americans cooked the redbud seedpods and ate the raw flowers.

Redbud trees are widely planted as ornamentals. In full bloom they are easy to spot while you're driving. Bright pink drifts along roadsides and front-yard specimens really stand out in the landscape.

Redbud is cauliflorous, meaning its flowers bloom directly on the branches and main trunk. This distinctive feature appears odd to many people when they first see the tree close up. Cauliflory is uncommon. Redbuds may have evolved this trait to provide easier access to insect pollinators that live near ground level.

Redbud flowers are nutritious. They contain more vitamin C than oranges on a weight basis (69–82 mg per 100 g). The purple-red color of the flowers comes from anthocyanins, a group of pigments that act as antioxidants and may reduce risk of cancer and cardiovascular disease.

Cherokee and other Native American tribes used the bark to treat coughs, diarrhea, fever, and vomiting. Flowering branches were brought into the home to "drive winter out." Redbud flowers were eaten by Cherokee children.

The beautiful flowers of redbud are antioxidant rich.

The species name *Cercis* is from the Greek *kerkis*, meaning "weaver's shuttle," referring to the shape of the pod. *Canadensis* means "of Canada." Southern Ontario is within the eastern redbud's native range.

Redbud flowers are an early nectar source for the ruby-throated hummingbird and for other pollinators, including several butterfly species. The seeds are relished by goldfinches, chickadees, and other birds. White-tailed deer browse the foliage and twigs.

Eastern redbud is a relatively short-lived tree, with a lifespan of twenty to twenty-five years. It self-seeds readily, and tiny redbud seedlings can often be found near the parent tree.

Spring beauty is a lovely little spring ephemeral.

## SPRING BEAUTY
*Claytonia virginica*

**Family:** Montiaceae
**Also called:** Grass-flower, fairy spuds, Virginia spring beauty
**Uses:** Entire plant is edible.
**Cautions:** Harvest sustainably. Possible look-alike species.
**Season:** Spring
**Range:** Throughout New Jersey and Pennsylvania; common in moist woods, fields, along streams, wetlands
**Description:** Delicate plant, 4"–8" high, with a pair of opposite grasslike leaves halfway up the stem. The sweet-scented flowers bloom late March through early May. They are less than ½" across, with 5 white petals, each veined with pink. Root a roundish corm, up to 2" in diameter with a dark brown covering.

Spring beauty is a short-lived wildflower, one of the earliest to emerge in spring. The plant takes advantage of the sunlight available before the trees leaf out. Considered a spring ephemeral, it quickly produces flowers and seeds to complete its life cycle in a brief period in spring.

The whole plant can be eaten, raw or cooked. Native people including the Iroquois and Algonquin valued spring beauties as food and stored the roots for winter use. Also known as "fairy spuds," the small potato-like roots can be boiled, roasted, or eaten raw. When boiled and dressed in a bit of butter, I find them sweet, chewy, and absolutely delicious. The starchy roots are a rich source of vitamins A and C and carbohydrate calories.

That said, sustainable foraging is an issue that should be considered. Some people question whether spring beauties and similar native species should ever be removed from the wild. In some places, it is quite plentiful. I have seen stunningly vast expanses of spring beauty, including a field of thousands on a campus in central Pennsylvania. If spring beauty populations are not abundant, they should not be disturbed. But if a plant is extremely plentiful, I see little harm in mindful harvesting of modest amounts where foraging is permitted. Nature affords plant species that provide nutrition and are meant as food for humans and other animals.

Growing your own supply of spring beauties may be the best way to go. They are easy to grow in a home garden, and like sun to partial shade. The roots, or corms, should only be purchased from reputable native plant nurseries.

In his book *Stalking the Wild Asparagus*, famous forager Euell Gibbons wrote about his fondness for fairy spuds. He enjoyed them "fried, mashed, in salads, and cooked with peas, like new potatoes," but said he preferred them simply "boiled in the jackets."

Gibbons also cautioned against greediness and recommended harvesting from areas where the flower is very abundant, collecting only larger roots and

The starchy roots of spring beauty are known as fairy spuds.

Fairy spuds boiled and buttered are delicious.

replanting the smaller ones. When harvesting spring beauty, make sure you don't take other plant roots growing nearby. When digging, follow the flower stem down until you reach a corm.

A possible look-alike plant is star-of-Bethlehem (*Ornithogalum umbellatum*), but if you look closely, the two are very different. Spring beauty has five petals, and star-of-Bethlehem has six. Also, star-of-Bethlehem petals have a green stripe on the back, and there is often a white line down the middle of each leaf.

Spring beauty is pollinated by a variety of bees, and there is one that needs it to survive. The spring beauty bee (*Andrena erigeniae*) collects pollen only from spring beauties. They can sometimes be seen with the pink pollen adorning their legs. The distinctive veins on the flower petals act as guides for bees, leading them to the center of the flower.

## RECIPE

**Fairy Spuds**

Spring beauty corms
Butter

Scrub the corms to remove most of the dirt. Boil until fork-tender, 10 minutes or more, depending on size. Drain, slip off the skins, and dip in melted butter.

The distinctive pink veins of spring beauty

A number of species of spring beauty grow in North America. Carolina spring beauty, *C. caroliniana,* is sometimes found in Pennsylvania; it also has edible spuds. The flowers are very similar, but the leaves are shorter and rounder than the far more common *C. virginica.* A rare yellow variety known as Hammond's yellow spring beauty (*C. virginica* var. *hammondiae*) is found in a protected area of New Jersey, in the foothills of the Kittatinny Mountains. This plant grows no place else on Earth. We will, of course, not be foraging this one!

Spruce tips are the new spring growth on spruce branches.

## SPRUCE
*Picea* spp.

**Family:** Pinaceae
**Also called:** Norway spruce, white spruce, black spruce, red spruce, blue spruce
**Uses:** Young shoots and cones, sap, inner bark
**Cautions:** Look-alike species
**Season:** Spring
**Range:** Throughout New Jersey and Pennsylvania; widely planted as ornamentals
**Description:** Evergreen tree with a pyramidal shape. Needles are short, 4-sided, and sharply pointed; they grow around the twig, each attached singly by a small peg-like structure. Cones are brown, woody.

Spring is the perfect time of year for gathering early wild greens, but we don't usually think of picking them from trees. Spruce trees give us that opportunity. The new young growth at the end of a spruce branch, called a spruce tip, is a tasty source of nourishment. Resembling the tip of a paintbrush, a spruce tip consists of compressed immature needles that will eventually grow and harden.

Spruce tips are lighter and brighter in color than the rest of the branch. To harvest, simply pick tips from the branches. Fresh shoots may still be partially enclosed in a papery covering. If so, just remove it. As tips emerge from their papery casings, they are at their best—tender, with a fruity lemony flavor and a hint of resin. As the needles get longer and start to fan out, they become more resinous. Taste as you harvest to get an idea of the flavor, which can vary from tree to tree.

A common use is spruce tip tea, made by steeping tips in boiled water and sweetening as desired. The tips can be added to savory dishes such as salads and cooked vegetables, as well as sweet creations. Chopped and baked into cookies or shortbread, spruce tips add a bright citrusy note. To preserve the flavor of spruce beyond the spring season, make spruce tip syrup.

There are approximately forty species of spruce worldwide, and all are safe to consume. The needles are rich in flavonoids, vitamin C, and other protective antioxidants. When harvesting, bear in mind that removing the tip is actually pruning that branch of the tree.

Little red male cones can be eaten right from the tree.

Norway spruce trees with graceful branches

Spruce was a staple in the diet of Native American tribes. Infusions of the needles and twigs were used to prevent scurvy. The shoots of various spruce species have been used since colonial days to flavor spruce beer. Captain James Cook provided his crew with spruce beer to fend off scurvy on long sea voyages.

Spruce sap, or resin, has been used since ancient times to treat sores and infected wounds. Native Americans used it as an analgesic, applying it as a poultice for boils and abscess pain. Modern research has demonstrated antibacterial activity of spruce resin, which may support its traditional use for treatment of skin wounds.

The inner bark of the tree was also eaten and served as an important emergency food source. Hardened spruce sap was chewed by both indigenous people and early settlers. The first chewing gum sold commercially was made from spruce resin, in the state of Maine in the mid-1800s.

Another edible spruce product is the little male cones. The roundish red cones are found in mid-spring on the lower branches. They are soft and mild tasting and are fun to eat directly from the tree or prepared in the same fashion as spruce tips. The green female cones are high up in the tree and, while edible, are much less accessible.

Norway spruce is the most commonly planted spruce in the area. It can be recognized by its graceful main branches, drooping branchlets, and large cones. Less common are the native white, black, and red spruces. Blue spruce is a landscape ornamental. All have similar edible and nutritional properties.

One evergreen, the yew (*Taxus* spp.), is a possible look-alike. Yew needles, however, are flattened, unlike the needles of spruce, which are four-sided and can be rolled between the fingers. Yew has fleshy red berries, which are actually a type of cone. Yew leaves and seeds are poisonous.

Stinging nettle with opposite leaves, stinging hairs, and serrated leaf edges

## STINGING NETTLE
*Urtica dioica*

**Family:** Urticaceae
**Also called:** Nettles, common nettle
**Uses:** Leaves, cooked
**Cautions:** Skin irritation, welts. Use during pregnancy is not advised.
**Season:** Late winter, spring
**Range:** Throughout New Jersey and Pennsylvania; near streams, moist woods, along trails, disturbed areas
**Description:** Stinging hairs on leaves and stems. Leaves opposite, roughly textured, lance shaped or somewhat heart shaped, 2"–5" long, tapered to a sharp tip, edges sharply serrated. Small greenish flowers hang in clusters from leaf axils. Plant 2'–6' tall.

Stinging nettle is considered a bothersome plant that can cause a nasty rash. The entire plant is armed with stinging hairs that inject an irritating chemical cocktail into the skin on contact. But once blanched or cooked, heat deactivates the sting, turning nettles into a delicious wild vegetable. Just take precautions when handling the plant.

Nettles are nutrient-dense and have been used for food since ancient times. A 100 g serving (½ cup cooked) provides your daily vitamin A requirement, along with significant amounts of fiber, potassium, calcium, iron, manganese, riboflavin, protein, and other nutrients.

The plant is widely considered medicinal, and some purported remedies are backed by modern research. Stinging nettle root is commonly marketed for enlarged prostate. Research suggests that it can ease the symptoms of this condition.

The best time to harvest nettles is late winter and early spring. Many sources state that nettles should be harvested before the plant flowers. Supposedly, older plants develop gritty particles called cystoliths that can irritate the kidneys. I have not been able to find any scientific evidence to support this. While it may very well be one of those myths that are repeated time and time again, err on the safe side and stick with the younger growth. Use of stinging nettles during pregnancy is controversial, so it's best to avoid.

Harvest the upper parts of young plants. Back in the kitchen, give them a good rinse, and remove leaves from the stems (with gloved hands). A brief submersion in boiling water is all it takes to remove the sting. Season and enjoy as a side dish, or chop and add to casseroles, etc. Stinging nettle makes a nice springtime soup, and an infusion of the leaves yields a good tea.

Nettle rennet is sometimes used in place of animal rennet to coagulate milk and produce cheese, a plant-based option acceptable to vegetarians.

There are two look-alike plants that are safe to eat. Wood nettle (*Laportea canadensis*) also has stinging hairs. Clearweed (*Pilea pumila*) has leaves and stems that appear translucent. False nettle (*Boehmeria cylindrica*) is not considered edible. It looks similar to stinging nettle, but does not have stinging hairs. White snakeroot (*Ageratina altissima*) has a similar appearance but is toxic. White snakeroot does not have hairs on the stems.

Stinging nettle is a nutrient-dense vegetable.

Stinging nettle in March

**Creamed Nettles on Toast**

4 cups chopped stinging nettles
2 tablespoons butter
2 cloves garlic, chopped
¼ cup cream
Sprinkle of nutmeg
Salt and pepper
Toasted bread

With gloved hands, add nettles to a pot of simmering water and cook for 5 minutes. Scoop the cooked nettles out into a large bowl. Save the cooking liquid—it's nettle tea! Rinse nettles in cold water, then squeeze handfuls to remove excess water. Heat a skillet over medium heat and add the butter and garlic. Cook until golden, about 3 minutes. Add nettles, cream, and nutmeg. Heat through. Season to taste and serve over toast.

A bowlful of freshly washed stinging nettle tops

So look for the stinging hairs. To be certain, there's always the "crash course" method of identifying stinging nettle: touching the leaves lightly with a finger. Many people have told me that this is what they did to make sure they had the right plant. There is no other plant in the United States that has this stinging effect.

The discomfort of stinging nettle is temporary and not horribly painful, and intentional exposure is actually a common practice for arthritis relief. The practice of urtication, or intentionally applying fresh nettles to the skin, is a folk remedy that has been practiced by many cultures. It is thought to improve blood circulation and help with the pain of arthritis and other ills. There is much anecdotal evidence and some scientific research supporting such use for joint pain. Studies have demonstrated that application of a stinging nettle cream was effective in reducing the pain of osteoarthritis.

Like other spring ephemerals, trout lily appears for a brief time in early spring.

# TROUT LILY
## *Erythronium americanum*

**Family:** Liliaceae
**Also called:** American trout lily, eastern trout lily, fawn lily, dogtooth violet, adder's tongue, lamb's tongue
**Uses:** Entire plant, raw or cooked
**Cautions:** No poisonous look-alikes. Emetic if consumed in large quantity; bulb may cause dermatitis to sensitive skin.
**Season:** Spring
**Range:** Throughout New Jersey and Pennsylvania; common in moist deciduous woods; found in colonies; prefers shade
**Description:** Small perennial herb with 1 or 2 leaves. Lance-shaped leaves up to 6" long and 2" wide with smooth margins; upper surface is mottled with brown or purplish markings, and lower surface is solid green. Younger nonflowering plants have a single leaf; mature flowering plants will grow 2 leaves. A single yellow flower is produced on a thin stalk. Flower is showy, nodding, and develops into an egg-shaped seed capsule. The root, a tiny corm, is less than ½" long.

Trout lily is a short-lived spring ephemeral of eastern woodlands that boasts a showy yellow lily-like flower. Like other ephemerals, trout lily appears for a brief time in early spring, disappearing by the time the trees leaf out.

The leaves of this native wildflower have spots that resemble the markings of a brook trout, hence the common name. The name dogtooth violet refers to the underground bulb thought to look like a dog's tooth. The petals are reflexed (curved backward) on sunny days, and the flowers close at night and on cloudy days.

The flavor of the tiny bulbs, called corms, is usually described as mild or sweet, and the texture is somewhat potato-like. The bulbs can be dug up, cleaned, and eaten raw, boiled, or roasted. The outer skin is tan, and the starchy inner flesh is white. The skin is usually discarded when eating.

The bulbs of all *Erythronium* species are considered edible. Native Americans and European colonists ate trout lily and stored the bulbs for winter food. There are at least twenty-seven species worldwide, and they have been a source of nourishment in other countries as well, including Russia's Siberia, China, and Japan.

Keep in mind that digging up the bulb kills the plant, so only harvest if very abundant. Sustainable foraging matters. Another reason to limit foraging of trout lily is that the entire plant is considered emetic, meaning it can make you vomit. Don't eat large amounts.

While nutritional analysis on this plant is scarce, trout lily may have some medicinal value. It is believed to have antibiotic properties, and according to modern research, water extracts of trout lily have been shown active against both gram-positive and gram-negative bacteria.

Trout lilies were used by various tribes of the eastern United States as both food and medicine. Juice from the leaves was used to treat wounds that wouldn't heal. The root was used for fever and for removing splinters. Women ate the leaves to prevent conception.

Trout lily leaves resemble the markings of a brook trout.

On sunny days, trout lily flowers open and the petals curve back.

The flowers are pollinated by bees and flies, and ants play an important role in the dispersal of trout lily seeds.

Violets are small but showy wildflowers.

# VIOLETS
*Viola* spp.

**Family:** Violaceae
**Also called:** Wild violet, common blue violet, woolly blue violet, confederate violet, door-yard violet, wood violet, meadow violet, garden violet, sweet violet
**Uses:** Flowers and leaves, raw or cooked
**Cautions:** Possible laxative
**Season:** Flowers in spring; leaves through summer
**Range:** Throughout New Jersey and Pennsylvania; meadows, lawns, woods, trailsides; sun to dappled shade
**Description:** Low-growing plant 6"–8" high. Leaves typically heart shaped with scalloped edges. Flowers are purple, blue, violet, white, yellow, or multicolored. They are bilaterally symmetrical, with 2 upper petals and 2 side petals; the lower petal is marked with veins and forms a spur.

Violets are one of our most familiar and easily recognized wildflowers. If you find wild violets in your lawn or garden, they are likely *V. sororia*. This native, often referred to as common blue violet, is the most common northeastern violet, and the state flower of New Jersey. Its scentless blooms most often appear in various shades of blue to purple but can be white. New leaves are tightly curled and will unfurl as they mature.

The many types of violets include species with yellow flowers and those with fragrant blooms.

White, purple, and yellow violets are all edible.

The leaves and flowers of all violet species are edible. There are more than 400 species worldwide, and it is not always easy to identify them, as they hybridize freely. In gardens, violets are often seen as "weedy." They grow in abundance when they like their location. The plant has been appreciated since ancient times for its beauty as well as its edible and medicinal value.

Analysis of common violet leaves reveals remarkably high levels of vitamin A (beta-carotene), much greater than that of spinach. One ounce of the leaves contains more than the full daily recommended allowance. They are similarly rich in vitamin C, having more than oranges by weight.

Veins on the lower petal direct insects to the nectar.

Young violet leaves are mild and can be enjoyed in salad. They are also cooked as a green vegetable and used to thicken soups. Mature foliage can be stringy, so steep older leaves for a vitamin C–rich tea.

Violets are one of the most popular edible flowers. Candied violets have been prepared in Europe for hundreds of years as an elegant garnish for cakes.

Cherokee people made various preparations of the plant to treat coughs, colds, and headache. Europeans have employed *Viola* species as a traditional remedy for skin conditions. The anti-inflammatory properties of the violet plant are at least partly attributed to salicylic acid, which is an aspirin-like compound, and rutin.

Violet leaves and flowers contain significant amounts of rutin, an antioxidant thought to strengthen blood vessels. Rutin supplements are popularly used for varicose veins, hemorrhoids, blood clot prevention, and arthritis.

The leaves may be somewhat laxative, so it is best to eat only smaller amounts at first to gauge tolerance. Anecdotes suggest that yellow-flowered varieties are more laxative than others. Violet roots are emetic and are not considered edible.

Violets are pollinated by winged insects, usually bees. The dark-colored veins on the lower petal act as a landing strip for the insects, directing them to the nectar at the flower's center.

Do not confuse wild violets with African violets. Those fuzzy-leaved houseplants are not violets at all and are not edible.

Harvesting violet leaves when the plant is in flower will help avoid confusion with lesser celandine (*Ficaria verna*), a toxic plant with dark green, fleshy, kidney-shaped leaves. Lesser celandine's symmetrical yellow flowers look nothing like violet flowers.

Grasslike clumps of wild garlic in spring

## WILD GARLIC
*Allium vineale*

**Family:** Amaryllidaceae
**Also called:** Crow garlic, field garlic
**Uses:** Whole plant edible, raw or cooked
**Cautions:** Look-alike plants
**Season:** Fall through spring
**Range:** Throughout New Jersey and Pennsylvania; lawns, fields, disturbed areas, edges of woods; sun to part shade
**Description:** Perennial plant. Leaves are long, thin, round, and hollow, up to 18" long. Usually grows in clumps. Entire plant has strong garlic or onion smell when crushed. Purplish flowers form at the top of a central stem; flowers may be replaced by aerial bulblets. Underground bulbs are white, round to oval, with a papery skin.

Wild garlic is a common member of the *Allium* genus, a huge group of more than 600 plants that includes onion, garlic, chives, and leeks.

Wild garlic is easy to find. In springtime it often appears in lawns as unruly grasslike clumps growing taller than the surrounding grass. Closer inspection

Aerial bulblets sprouting "hair"

reveals that, unlike grass, the leaves are hollow and give off an unmistakable onion/garlic odor when broken.

The long slender leaves resemble chives and can be used in much the same way. The snipped leaves add flavor and nutrition to salads, potatoes, pasta, and egg dishes. The bulbs can be used in recipes as you would supermarket garlic.

Wild garlic flowers are also edible. If left on the plant, the flower may produce bulblets, which can form a new plant when they fall to the soil. Often the bulblets sprout while still on the plant; the result is rather bizarre, resembling a little purple head with wiry green hair.

Wild garlic is widely naturalized and quite plentiful, so don't worry about overharvesting. It can even be found in winter, the green tufts contrasting with drab leaf litter.

April and May yield the plumpest bulbs. To get the most bang for your foraging buck, look for the largest, thickest plants and pull each one up individually. Grasp the plant at ground level and pull straight up. Using two hands gives you a better chance of getting the intact plant with bulb. You could dig up the entire clump, but this is more work, since you would be sorting through the clod of dirt to discard the tiniest bulbs.

To process wild garlic, trim off the roots, rinse the plants, then strip away any papery outer skin. Now separate your wild garlic into its two useful parts: the greens and the bulbs. The bulbs have a more pronounced flavor than the leaves, and cooking will mellow the flavor. Bulbs may occasionally form small cloves attached to the main bulb; these are fine to eat.

**Penne with Wild Garlic and Cheese**

12 ounces penne pasta
¼ cup olive oil
⅓ cup wild garlic bulbs, trimmed
¼ teaspoon red pepper flakes
½ cup grated Parmesan cheese
Salt and pepper to taste

Cook the pasta according to package directions. Drain, reserving 1 cup of the cooking water. Return the pasta to the pot. Stir in ¼ cup of the reserved water, and put the lid on. In a skillet, heat the oil. Add the wild garlic and pepper flakes. Sauté until garlic is golden. Remove skillet from heat. Add the oil and garlic to the pasta. Mix in the Parmesan. Stir in enough reserved water to make just a little broth. Add salt and pepper to taste.

The green tufts of wild garlic stand out in the winter landscape.

Wild garlic plants, washed and ready to go

Wild garlic contains a variety of sulfur compounds, which give the plant its characteristic pungent aroma. These compounds have shown antifungal, antibacterial, and antiviral properties. Wild garlic leaves possess significant antioxidant activity, which is attributed to high levels of vitamin C, carotenoids, flavonoids, and chlorophyll.

Native Americans used the plant as a diuretic, as an expectorant, and to treat scurvy. *A. vineale* is native to Europe, North Africa, and the Middle East. It has a long history of use in those countries.

A good rule of thumb: If the plant looks like onion or garlic and it smells like onion or garlic, it is safe to eat. There are look-alike plants to be aware of, however. Star-of-Bethlehem (*Ornithogalum umbellatum*) is a garden escapee with leaves bearing a distinct white midvein, which wild garlic lacks. The death camas plant (*Toxicoscordion* or *Zigadenus* spp.) might be mistaken for wild garlic at first glance, but death camas leaves have parallel veins, and the leaves are not hollow. Always check for the hollow leaves and the distinctive onion/garlic smell. As always, when in doubt, don't eat it.

Wintercress has bright yellow four-petaled flowers.

## WINTERCRESS
*Barbarea vulgaris*

**Family:** Brassicaceae
**Also called:** Yellow rocket
**Uses:** Leaves, buds, tender stems, and flowers
**Cautions:** No look-alikes of concern
**Season:** Late winter, spring
**Range:** Throughout New Jersey and Pennsylvania; along streams, edges of woods, roadsides, in fields and moist areas
**Description:** Herbaceous biennial plant. Basal rosette of leaves that are deeply lobed, dark green, smooth, and glossy. Each has a terminal lobe that is much larger than the small paired lobes below. Lower leaves have petioles. Upper leaves are much smaller and clasp the stem. Stems are 1'–2' tall and solid, not hollow. Small flower bud clusters appear at top of stem; buds open to yellow 4-petaled flowers.

From mid-spring to early summer, the vivid yellow blooms of wintercress brighten fields and roadsides. During this time, wintercress, so named because it survives over winter, explodes its color onto the landscape.

Wintercress has the ability to hunker down and survive winter's freezing temperatures. When warm weather arrives, it bounces back and resumes rapid growth. Soon the plant goes vertical, putting up stems that produce small clusters of flower buds at the tips.

Take the top 3 inches or so of bud clusters, stem, and smaller leaves.

At this early flower bud stage, wintercress is prime for eating. The top few inches of the plant easily becomes a fabulous cooked vegetable. The closed buds look somewhat like tiny broccoli heads and are bitter when raw. Most people find wintercress too bitter unless properly cooked to mellow the flavor. When lightly cooked in water, wintercress is completely transformed. I remember being shocked the first time I ate the blanched and buttered buds. They were so mild and tasty, I wished I had picked more.

To harvest, snap off wintercress bud clusters along with about 3 inches or so of tender stem and smaller leaves. If the buds have started to open and a few flowers appear, that's fine. Treat wintercress bud clusters as you would broccoli, but cook for a shorter time since it's a more tender veggie.

In addition to the flower buds, the basal leaves foraged in late winter and early spring can be prepared in the same manner. Pick them from the plant

RECIPE

**Simply Delicious Wintercress Buds**

Bring a pot of water to a boil. Add wintercress bud clusters, reduce heat to simmer, and cook gently for 2 minutes, uncovered. Taste a piece. If not mild enough, cook for another minute or so. Drain and add a dab of butter. Wintercress is delicious with little more, but other flavoring options include salt, pepper, a sprinkle of lemon juice, or herbs of choice.

Wintercress buds are a delicious wild vegetable.

one by one. Let your taste buds dictate whether they are suitable for eating raw or need to be cooked.

Wintercress is a member of the mustard family, which also includes broccoli, kale, radishes, bok choy, and cabbage. All vegetables in this group contain glucosinolates, plant chemicals that are very strongly associated with protection against cancer. These sulfur compounds are also responsible for the characteristic hot, pungent flavor of mustard-family vegetables. Wintercress is also rich in vitamins A and C.

Look-alike mustard plants are edible, so there is no problem in mistaking one for another. One example is upland cress (*B. verna*), a popular wild green of southern states fondly known as creasy greens. Another is watercress (*Nasturtium officinale*), a peppery tasting green that grows in wetter habitats.

Native to Europe and Asia, wintercress has a history of culinary use by many cultures, including Native Americans. The plant is widely naturalized across the United States.

Young basal leaves of wintercress. Note the large terminal lobes.

# Plants of Summer

Beach plums look like tiny plums. They are usually purple but can be blue, red, or nearly black.
KAREN CARLOUGH

## BEACH PLUM
*Prunus maritima*

**Family:** Rosaceae

**Also called:** Shore plum, seaside plum, sand plum

**Uses:** Fruit raw, dried, or cooked

**Cautions:** No poisonous look-alikes. Seeds should not be eaten.

**Season:** Late summer

**Range:** Abundant along the New Jersey shore; grows on sand dunes and in rocky or sandy soils. This is an endangered species in Pennsylvania.

**Description:** A dense shrub typically 3'–6' tall. The fruit is a small round plum, ½"–1" in diameter on a short stem. Usually purple, the fruit can also be blue, red, or nearly black; rarely yellow. Deep purple when ripe. A thin layer of flesh surrounds a large stone. Covered with a whitish waxy coating (bloom) that can be rubbed off. Leaves are 2"–3" long, alternate, oval, serrated along edges, with a pointed tip. They are smooth on top, with downy undersides. Small fragrant 5-petaled white flowers appear before the leaves in spring. Plant is thornless.

Wild beach plums grow in the sandy soils of the Atlantic coast from Maine to Virginia. Looking like tiny cultivated plums, beach plums can be eaten out of hand, although they tend to be pretty sour. They are usually made into jam, jelly, pie, and other recipes that call for a good amount of sugar.

The native plums are typically found on dunes and sandy beaches, but they sometimes thrive inland along roadsides and in sandy fields. Much beach plum habitat has been lost to development, but the plant still grows abundantly on the sandy beaches of New Jersey, especially in Cape May County. Beach plum plants are known for having years in which they bear little or no fruit, and may have a pattern of bearing every other year. A beach plum festival is held each year at Island Beach State Park in Ocean County, New Jersey, to celebrate the fruit.

Although Pennsylvania does not border the Atlantic, there are rare native populations of beach plums growing in red shale areas of Bucks and Montgomery Counties. The plant is an endangered species in the state.

Beach plums were one of the first plants noticed by European explorers when they came ashore. The fruits were used by indigenous peoples and by early colonists, who cooked them into jams, jellies, puddings, cakes, and other dishes and dried them for storage.

Beach plums are health protective. They are rich in antioxidants and contain proanthocyanidins. These powerful substances, also found in cranberries and blueberries, are being researched for antibacterial properties and their potential to reduce cardiovascular disease and cancer risk.

Beach plum pits contain hydrocyanic acid, which is toxic. However, it is safe to cook the fruit along with the pits and strain them out afterward.

The fruits freeze well. If you happen to have an abundance of them, you can store whole, unpitted beach plums in freezer bags or containers. They will keep

Beach plums growing on the beaches of Sandy Hook, New Jersey KAREN CARLOUGH

**Beach Plum Juice**

4–5 cups whole beach plums, rinsed and stemmed
1 cup water
Sugar to taste

Put the beach plums and the water in a large saucepan. Crush the plums to release their juices (a potato masher works for this). Simmer uncovered 15–20 minutes, stirring occasionally, until fruit is soft. Remove from heat. To strain juice from the pulp, pass it through a jelly bag or a fine strainer. This is basic beach plum juice. Sweeten to taste.

for at least 6 months. As with regular plums, beach plums can also be dried to create beach prunes.

Wild beach plum plants are very hardy, thriving in adverse conditions of nutrient-poor soil, high salt levels, high winds, and blowing, shifting sand, which often buries the plants. The deep roots help to stabilize sand dunes, and beach plum is sometimes planted in conservation efforts to prevent beach erosion.

Beach plums are an important food source for wildlife and migratory birds.

Beach plums are an important food source for migratory birds. KAREN CARLOUGH

The bark of the mature black cherry resembles burnt cornflakes.

## BLACK CHERRY
*Prunus serotina*

**Family:** Rosaceae
**Also called:** Wild black cherry, rum cherry, wild cherry, cabinet cherry
**Uses:** Flesh of ripe fruit, raw or cooked
**Cautions:** Do not consume the leaves, twigs, bark, or seeds.
**Season:** Summer, early fall
**Range:** Throughout New Jersey and Pennsylvania; forests, woodlands, thickets
**Description:** Medium to large deciduous tree. Leaves are simple, alternate, 3"–5" long, finely serrated with in-curved teeth. Older leaves will have whitish or rust colored hairs along the midrib on the back of the leaf. Flowers and fruits grow in an elongated raceme. Flowers are white. Fruit is round, purple-black when ripe, about ⅓" across, with a thin layer of soft flesh around a single round, hard pit. Tree has no thorns. Bark is dark reddish brown to nearly black. Young bark has horizontal lenticels; older bark becomes scaly and resembles burnt cornflakes.

The fruit of native black cherry is small. When fully ripe, the cherries are tart but richly flavored. They are sometimes described as bittersweet. While not luxuriously fleshy and sweet like their cultivated cousins in the produce aisle, the pea-size fruits are still a treat.

Pioneers used wild black cherries to flavor rum and make a drink called cherry bounce, hence the common name rum cherry. Menominee Indians were said to have gotten intoxicated by consuming the fruit, which was allowed to

**Black Cherry Sauce**

1 cup wild black cherries (can be cooked with the pits and separated later)
2–3 tablespoons sugar

Put cherries in a small saucepan. Add water to just cover. Bring to a boil, then reduce to a simmer. Cook 20 minutes with the lid slightly ajar, stirring once or twice. Remove the lid and simmer until cherries are very soft and most of the liquid is evaporated. Let cool slightly. Put the fruit into a sieve placed over a bowl. Press to separate out juice and pulp. Discard the pits. Add sugar to taste. If desired, the sauce can be thickened further by heating again.

stand and ferment. Native peoples also dried the flesh of wild cherries and added it to pemmican, a dried food mix roughly equivalent to a modern energy bar.

In recipes, the tart quality of the fruit is usually balanced with added sugar. Popular uses include jams, juice, syrups, and sauces.

A raceme of black cherries, mostly ripe

To harvest, pick cherries straight from the tree. Choose only the ripe ones, which should be soft and dark purple-black. Fruits start to ripen in mid- to late summer and can even be found in early fall if the birds haven't devoured them all. Only the flesh is edible, so spit out the pit, just like with ordinary cherries.

Black cherry fruits are a rich source of natural antioxidants. They have a high content of phenolic compounds, which have been shown to have antihypertensive activity. Analysis also reveals high levels of protein, vitamin C, calcium, potassium, and magnesium.

Native Americans made infusions of black cherry bark for fever, colds, and cough. Bark extract of *P. serotina* is still used in natural over-the-counter cough syrups, and specific methods of preparation and dosage must be adhered to. Consumption of the bark is beyond the scope of this book and is not recommended due to risk of toxicity.

Black cherry twigs give off a strong almond odor when broken or scratched. This odor is produced by cyanogenic glycosides and is one way to identify the species. Livestock and pets have been poisoned by eating the tree's bark, roots, and leaves.

Black cherry has become invasive in Europe since its introduction there as an ornamental in the seventeenth century. The fruits are eagerly sought by birds, and are also food for black bears, turkeys, and raccoons. Black knot, a fungal disease, is common; the dark, warty growths can often be seen scattered throughout the branches.

Black cherries are relished by birds and other wildlife.

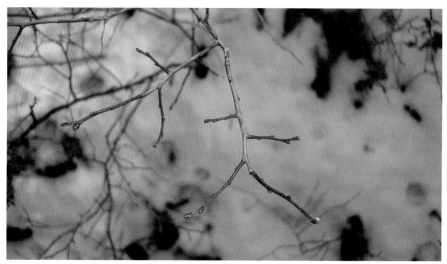
Winter twigs of blueberry

## BLUEBERRY
*Vaccinium* spp.

**Family:** Ericaceae
**Also called:** Wild blueberry; sometimes called huckleberries, although they are botanically distinct species.
**Uses:** Berries fresh or cooked; leaves for tea
**Cautions:** No poisonous look-alikes. Blueberry allergy is extremely rare.
**Season:** Berries mid- to late summer; leaves when available
**Range:** Throughout New Jersey and Pennsylvania
**Description:** Perennial shrub. Highbush blueberry is 6'–12' tall, leaf edge smooth or serrated. Lowbush species are 6"–2', with smaller berries, leaves very finely serrated. All blueberry fruit is blue-purple with a calyx. Twigs have a zigzag appearance; leaves are alternate along the twigs. Twigs turn reddish in winter. Flowers bell-shaped and white or pinkish white.

Even if the only blueberries you've seen are the cultivated types, you'll likely recognize the wild variety when you come across it. A wild blueberry will have that same rich blue-purple color when ripe and will be topped with the characteristic blueberry "crown," or calyx. Wild berries are usually smaller than their plump supermarket counterparts.

A number of native blueberries are found in the area. Lowbush blueberries, as the name implies, are small plants. They often form a woodland ground cover, and the berries tend to be tiny. Three types are lowbush blueberry (*V. pallidum*), low sweet blueberry (*V. angustifolium*), and sourtop blueberry (*V. myrtilloides*), which is uncommon. A tall variety called highbush blueberry (*V. corymbosum* or *V. caesariense*) is found in bogs and other wet areas.

Modern cultivated blueberries were developed in the early 1900s in the Pine Barrens of New Jersey, when wild highbush blueberries were crossbred to develop large, consistently sweet berries for market. This resulted in the blueberries we know today. In 2004 the blueberry was named the state fruit of New Jersey.

Blueberries have long been an important food for humans. They were enjoyed in fresh, cooked, and dried form by Native Americans long before European contact. The dried fruit was added to pemmican, a nutrient-dense mixture of meat and animal fat that sustained people on long trips and provided nourishment through winter months.

Nutritionally, blueberries are truly a superfood. They are low in calories and rich in vitamins C and K and the mineral manganese. They have one of the highest antioxidant values of all foods. Antioxidants are natural substances that protect your body from free radicals, molecules that damage cells and can lead to disease. Blueberries contain an array of powerful substances that can help prevent chronic disease. One study involving more than 16,000

Unripe blueberries with the characteristic "crown"

Blueberries are devoured by birds as soon as they ripen.

participants found that antioxidants in blueberries appeared to slow the rate of cognitive decline in older adults.

Blueberry leaves may have even more potent health benefits than the fruits. A research study that prepared 30-minute infusions of blueberry leaves using methods that mimicked home brewing of tea showed that the resulting tea contained very high levels of antioxidants.

Blueberries (wild or store-bought) tend to have a whitish coating on them. This is a natural part of the fruit known as the bloom. It's a safe waxy substance that protects the berry from bacteria and helps seal in moisture.

Blueberries have no poisonous look-alikes. Huckleberries (*Gaylussacia* spp.) look like blueberries but have ten large seeds inside. They are perfectly edible. Serviceberries (*Amelanchier* spp.) also look very similar to blueberries. They are also edible (deliciously so). A serviceberry has a "crown" on one end, just like a blueberry.

Blueberries are relished by many birds, as well as mammals large and small.

Raspberries have a hollow, cuplike core.

## BRAMBLES
*Rubus* spp.

**Family:** Rosaceae

**Also called:** Blackberry, raspberry, black cap, wineberry, dewberry

**Uses:** Fruits, raw or cooked

**Cautions:** No look-alikes

**Season:** Summer

**Range:** Throughout New Jersey and Pennsylvania; along roadsides, hiking trails, edges of woods

**Description:** Shrub or vine with arching or sprawling prickly stems. Compound leaves, usually with 3–5 leaflets, alternate on the stem. Leaflet edges are serrated. Flowers have 5 petals and are usually pink or white. Fruit is a cluster of drupelets.

Brambles are thorny shrubs or vines that bear edible fruit. This large group of plants includes the foraged summertime favorites blackberries and raspberries. Although they are commonly called berries, bramble fruits are actually a cluster of tiny fruits called drupes, each containing one seed. Botanists refer to this as an aggregate fruit, or an aggregate of drupelets. In addition to the well-known blackberries and raspberries, other brambles include dewberries, loganberries, and cloudberries. It can be difficult to tell *Rubus* species apart, since they hybridize readily. Botanists recognize hundreds of brambles and do not agree on the exact number.

The wineberry plant is covered with reddish hairs.

Blackberries are purple-black when ripe. Harvest the darkest ones.

Dewberries are small plants.

Blackberries and raspberries are pretty easy to identify. A helpful rule of thumb: If a fruit looks like a raspberry or blackberry (i.e., an aggregate fruit) and is on a thorny shrub, you can eat it. All bramble fruits are nutritious, and most are sweet and tasty.

Wild raspberries can be red or black when ripe, depending on the type. All raspberries have a hollow core. The berry looks like a little cup, because it left its core behind on the plant. This is how you can tell a raspberry from a blackberry, which is not hollow or cuplike. Raspberry leaves are green above and silvery white below.

Our native black raspberry, *R. occidentalis*, is one of the finest wild fruits. Also known as black caps, they are purplish black when ripe and about ½ inch in diameter. The sweet, juicy fruits ripen in midsummer. The stem of black raspberry is round and usually has a bluish-white powdery coating called bloom, which you can easily rub off. The stem is protected by thorns along its length.

Red raspberries (*R. idaeus*) are red when ripe. The stems are round and have prickles but no powdery bloom. Red raspberries are less common than black raspberries, but they are equally delicious.

Another commonly foraged raspberry is the wineberry (*R. phoenicolasius*). Native to Asia, wineberry is considered invasive in our area. The fruit is red, juicy, and arguably the tastiest of raspberries. This very widespread bramble can be identified by the reddish hairs and spines that cover the stems.

Blackberries ripen a little later than raspberries. Blackberry thorns are larger than raspberry thorns, and the stems have grooves or ridges. Blackberries have a solid core. They turn purple-black when ripe.

Dewberries are closely related to blackberries. The dewberry plant is small, with stems that trail along the ground. Dewberries ripen in early summer, before raspberries. Ripe berries are purple-black and quite soft.

All bramble berries are antioxidant rich and nutritious, often more so than their cultivated counterparts. They are rich in vitamin C, anthocyanins, and other phenols. Such compounds help prevent cancer, heart disease, and hypertension, and have been shown to improve vision and memory.

If you find yourself with an abundance of berries, freeze them. Put them in a single layer on a baking tray lined with waxed paper. Freeze for at least 3 hours, then transfer berries into freezer bags or containers.

## RECIPE

**Brambleberry Rendezvous Ice Cream**

1½ quarts vanilla ice cream
1 cup chopped peanut butter cups
1½ cups wild raspberries or blackberries

Let the ice cream stand at room temperature to soften slightly. Scoop into a mixing bowl. Add peanut butter cups and berries. Use a rubber spatula to gently combine. Transfer ice cream mixture into a lidded container; freeze until firm.

Brambleberry ice cream is full of antioxidants!

Unopened milkweed flower buds

## COMMON MILKWEED
*Asclepias syriaca*

**Family:** Apocynaceae
**Also called:** Milkweed, silkweed, cottonweed
**Uses:** Cooked young shoots, buds, flowers, young seedpods
**Cautions:** Look-alike species
**Season:** Spring through summer
**Range:** Throughout New Jersey and Pennsylvania; sunny roadsides, fencerows, fields
**Description:** Herbaceous perennial, 3'–5' tall. Stems are thick, green, hollow, and slightly downy; they do not branch. The broad oblong leaves are opposite on the stem, up to 8" long and 3½" wide, with a short thick petiole and a smooth margin. Stems and leaves exude milky sap when broken. A ball of flower buds develops into a loose sphere of hourglass-shaped pink flowers. Bloom time is early to mid-summer. Some flowers become warty seedpods, which release seeds in the fall.

Common milkweed, native to the eastern United States, is one of our finest wild vegetables. The plant has been used as food for a long time. Indigenous peoples ate common milkweed. The shoots, tender leaves, flower buds, and immature seedpods were prepared in many ways, often cooked as greens or added to meat or soup. The flowers were used to make jam.

Milkweed, named for its milky sap, offers several edible parts. The first are the young spring shoots, harvested when up to 12–14 inches tall. Boil the shoots until tender, which may take at least 10 minutes. The immature leaves at the tip

**Sautéed Milkweed Pods**

Handful of young milkweed pods
Flour for coating
Olive oil or butter
Salt and pepper

Boil the pods for 3–4 minutes then drain, discarding the water. Pat the pods dry and dredge them in a little flour. Heat oil or butter in a skillet, and sauté the pods until golden. Season to taste. A delicious summer vegetable served hot or at room temperature.

are OK to eat. Drain the shoots, and discard the water. Season and enjoy as is, or use in recipes as you would asparagus.

The flower buds are my favorite. They look like little green peas but taste like green beans. Blanch the clusters for 2 minutes in boiling water, then dress simply and eat, or add to recipes such as soups or casseroles. The flower buds are high in protein (21 percent) and total dietary fiber (37 percent).

Fragrant pink milkweed flowers make a nice salad garnish. They also make lovely fritters. Just dip the flower cluster into pancake batter and fry in a little butter.

Milkweed flowers on the left; flower buds on the right

Young milkweed pods are a delicious wild vegetable.

The green immature pods are a satisfying and versatile vegetable. Harvest pods up to about 1½ inches. Pods up to 2 inches are usually still good. They should be solid not spongy, and white inside with no hint of brown. Mature pods have developed seeds and are not good for eating. Boil the young pods for a few minutes, then eat as a side dish or use in stir fries, stews, etc.

Common milkweed is vital to the survival of the monarch butterfly, as it is the main food for the larvae. Forage mindfully. Harvest only when plentiful, and take only a small percentage.

Misconceptions abound about the safety of eating milkweed. You may read that it needs to be boiled in multiple changes of water to eliminate bitter toxins. This myth has been repeated over and over. Common milkweed, *A. syriaca*, is not bitter. It is safe to eat when cooked once and does not require extreme measures. Boil the edible parts until tender, then taste. If it tastes OK, you're good to go. If it's bitter, just spit it out. It probably means you picked the wrong plant.

There are a number of milkweed species throughout the country, containing varying amounts of cardiac glycosides. Common milkweed has such a small amount of the bitter substance that it is hardly perceptible. The fallacies about eating milkweed are likely due to people who have eaten the wrong plant, probably dogbane (*Apocynum cannabinum*). Dogbane is somewhat toxic to humans,

Milkweed on the right; branching dogbane on the left

and the spring shoots are sometimes confused with milkweed. Dogbane has a solid stem; milkweed has a hollow stem. As the two plants mature, they are easy to tell apart. Milkweed stems are unbranched and have minute fuzz; dogbane stems branch, are smooth and hairless, and usually have reddish markings. Dogbane flowers are whitish green. The related butterfly weed (*A. tuberosa*) has yellow or orange flowers and does not have milky sap. Its edibility is questionable.

Native Americans used common milkweed for a variety of ailments. They applied the milky sap to remove warts, a folk remedy that remains in use today. The stems have been a source of fibers to make sewing thread, fishing line, and cordage.

In fall, when the dry milkweed pods split, they release seeds that are carried aloft by white silky fuzz. The buoyant silky fibers were used as a kapok substitute for life vests during World War II.

Cornelian cherry is a type of dogwood. You may see the similarity in the leaves.

## CORNELIAN CHERRY
*Cornus mas*

**Family:** Cornaceae
**Also called:** Cornelian cherry dogwood, European cornel
**Uses:** Fruit, raw or cooked
**Cautions:** No poisonous look-alikes
**Season:** September to October
**Range:** Throughout New Jersey and Pennsylvania as a planted ornamental; sometimes naturalized in woods
**Description:** Deciduous shrub or small tree, up to 25' tall. Fruit is red, fleshy, oblong, about ¾" long, with 1 large seed. Tiny clusters of small yellow flowers appear in spring, followed by the leaves. Leaves are opposite, 2"–4" long, ovate, entire.

Cornelian cherry is a fruit tree you are more likely to find in a park or on a college campus than in a wild setting. *Cornus mas* is native to southern Europe and western Asia, where it grows wild in forests. Its luscious fruits are widely foraged and cultivated in its native range. In the United States cornelian cherry occasionally appears in disturbed wooded areas, but you're more likely to find this tree planted as an attractive garden specimen.

Despite the name, cornelian cherry is not a cherry but a type of dogwood. When fully ripe, the cherrylike fruits are dark red in color and delicious. The fruits will fall from the tree when fully ripe. Before that point, they are quite sour.

Fully ripe fruits are dark in color and delicious.

To collect the ripe fruit, gather those that have fallen to the ground, or spread a blanket or tarp under the tree and gently shake the branches so the ripest fruits drop. If picked before fully sweet, just let them sit at room temperature for a couple of days.

Since ancient times, cornelian cherries have been valued as food and folk medicine. In Europe, Asia, and the Middle East, they have been used in treating of a wide range of conditions, such as fever, diabetes, diarrhea, gastrointestinal disorders, kidney and liver diseases, and urinary tract infections. The fruits are enjoyed in traditional recipes such as jam, juice, dried fruit, and pickled cherries.

The antioxidant-rich fruits are a significant source of vitamin C. Clinical trials have shown that cornelian cherries have potential for treating diabetes,

## RECIPE

**Cornelian Cherry Fruit Leather**

4 cups ripe cornelian cherries
1 cup water
Sugar to taste

Place the cherries and water in a saucepan. Bring to a simmer and cook, covered, until the fruit separates from the pit, about 30 minutes. Uncover and cook until most of the water evaporates. Remove from heat and allow to cool slightly. Press the fruit through a sieve. Discard the seeds. Add sugar to the pulp to taste. Process in a dehydrator according to manufacturer's directions.

Alternately, spread the pulp evenly onto a silicone or parchment-lined baking sheet and place in a low oven (170°F) until dried. Time will vary depending on thickness and moisture content; it will probably take at least 4 hours. When dry to the touch, peel the fruit leather off. Cut into strips and roll in plastic to store.

Cornelian cherries ripen over an extended period.

hyperlipidemia, and gastrointestinal disorders. Anthocyanins, which are responsible for the fruits' red color, have been found to increase as the fruits ripen and become darker. These natural pigments may reduce the risk of heart disease, cancer, and cognitive impairment.

The wood of cornelian cherry is very hard and has been valued for making tool handles, weapons, and wheel spokes. It is said that the legendary Trojan horse was built from cornelian cherry wood.

Another type of dogwood, the kousa, or Chinese dogwood (*C. kousa*), also has edible fruits. Like cornelian cherry, kousa has naturalized somewhat in the area, but it is found mainly as a planted specimen. Kousa fruit can be eaten raw and is sometimes made into jelly. The bright red, bumpy fruits have a lot of seeds. The skins are edible but have a gritty quality. When harvesting kousa, take fruits that are slightly soft to the touch.

The fruit of our native flowering dogwood (*C. florida*) is not edible. The small oval fruit has a thin layer of unpalatable flesh surrounding a large stone.

The edible fruit of kousa dogwood

Berries are dark and juicy when ripe, and should always be cooked.

## ELDERBERRY
*Sambucus canadensis* and *S. nigra*

**Family:** Adoxaceae
**Also called:** Black elderberry, common elderberry, sambucus, elder, elderblow
**Uses:** Flowers, cooked ripe berries
**Cautions:** Leaves, stems, bark, root, unripe and raw berries; possible look-alikes. Not recommended if pregnant/nursing or under 18 years of age.
**Season:** Late summer to early fall
**Range:** Throughout New Jersey and Pennsylvania; along roadsides, fields, forest edges
**Description:** Shrub to 10'–20' high. Pinnately compound green leaves are up to 12" long, each consisting of 3–7 serrated leaflets, to 6" long. Plant has no spines or thorns. Small white, sweet-scented flowers are borne in large flat-topped clusters up to 10" across. Bloom time is late spring, summer. Flower clusters develop into drooping deep purple berry clusters in late summer. Berries are tiny and round.

Elderberry is a lovely plant with a long history of use as food. American and European elderberry (*Sambucus canadensis* and *S. nigra*, respectively) are the two

Elder flower cluster

most common elderberry plants in the United States. They are closely related and are used in the same way.

Only the flowers and ripe berries can be eaten. When ripe, the berries will be soft, dark colored, and easily squished between the fingers. They should be cooked. The seeds contain glycosides that may cause nausea, but this substance is destroyed by cooking. Elderberry syrup, pie, wine, and jelly are popular recipes.

Elder flowers can be eaten raw or cooked. They are nice used as garnish. Dipping the flower clusters into batter to make elderberry fritters is arguably the finest thing you can do with them.

## RECIPE

**Elder Flower Fritters**

Elderberry flower clusters with stems, washed and patted dry
Batch of your favorite pancake batter (boxed mix is fine)
Oil for frying
Confectioners' sugar

Heat at least ½ inch oil in a heavy skillet or a deep-fat fryer. Using the stem as a handle, dip each cluster into the batter. Shake off excess batter, and carefully submerge the cluster into the hot oil. Fry until golden. Drain on paper towels. Dust fritters with confectioners' sugar. Discard the stems.

To harvest the flowers or berries, simply snip the cluster near the base. Berries can be frozen for later use, and freezing the clusters makes separating berries from stems an easier task.

Elderberry has traditionally been used to treat coughs, colds, fever, and aches, and as a laxative and diuretic. The flowers have been applied topically since ancient times to soothe skin, fade blemishes, and lighten freckles.

Elderberries are high in fiber, protein, and vitamin C. They are one of the most powerful antioxidant fruits. High levels of anthocyanins and flavonoids have been demonstrated, and these compounds are known to have significant antioxidant disease-fighting potential. Elderberries have shown potent antiviral activity in the lab, and studies have shown elderberry extract effective in alleviating symptoms of cold and flu.

The easiest time to identify elderberry is while it's in bloom. The showy white clusters are very large. If you intend to forage the flowers, be sure to identify the plant properly. There are reports of elder flowers being mistaken for those of the poisonous water hemlock (*Cicuta maculata*). Both plants have clusters of small white flowers. Water hemlock does not produce berries. It is an herbaceous plant, not woody like elderberry, which has bark on its trunk and branches, so look for the bark. The stem of water hemlock is purplish, or green with purple blotches. Water hemlock leaves are alternate; elderberry leaves are opposite.

Children have used hollowed elderberry stems as blowguns or whistles; this is not advised due to possible toxicity.

Elderberry is also sometimes confused with *Aralia spinosa* or *Aralia elata*. These plants have thorny stems and branches. Elderberry has no thorns.

Elder flower clusters can be up to 10 inches across.

Heal-all, not yet flowering

## HEAL-ALL
*Prunella vulgaris*

**Family:** Lamiaceae
**Also called:** Common self-heal, self-heal, woundwort, heart-of-the-earth, carpenter's herb
**Uses:** Whole plant; shoots and leaves, raw or cooked
**Cautions:** No look-alikes of concern. Safety during pregnancy/nursing is unknown.
**Season:** Spring, summer
**Range:** Throughout New Jersey and Pennsylvania; common in lawns, fields, gardens, along woodland edges
**Description:** Small perennial up to 12" tall. Lance-shaped leaves are opposite, up to 2½" long; leaf margins are entire (smooth) or slightly indented. Stems are square with dense cylindrical flower heads, which do not taper. Flower heads are about 1" long and appear in late spring. Flowers are tiny, purple, and snapdragon-like. They do not open simultaneously.

*Prunella vulgaris* has a long history of use around the world, both as an edible plant and as medicine. It is commonly known as heal-all or self-heal due to its widespread use in traditional medicine for various ailments. The leaves of the plant are very mild tasting, especially before the plant flowers. I like to eat the leaves as a trail nibble. Mature plants may be more astringent due to the presence of tannins. The flower heads are edible but not pleasant tasting. Tender leaves can be added to mixed salads or incorporated into soup, stews, casseroles, and other dishes. When cooked, heal-all can be seasoned in any number of ways.

The use of *P. vulgaris* has often focused on its reputation as a healing herb. It was used by numerous North American Indian tribes for a wide range of purposes. Cold-water infusions were used as a beverage; hot or cold tea was taken as a tonic. Cherokee people employed it as a burn dressing and for other skin conditions. The Iroquois used it as a general panacea, taken for coughs, colds, fever, treatment of tuberculosis, gastrointestinal ailments, and more.

Heal-all flowers starting to open

Heal-all was traditionally viewed in Europe as a remedy for sore throat and wound healing. The seventeenth-century English herbalist Nicholas Culpeper wrote of heal-all, "whereby when you are hurt you may heal yourself."

Therapeutic uses of heal-all may be supported by the presence of the many beneficial compounds that have been found in the plant, including carotene, vitamin C, vitamin K3, nicotinic acid, and thiamine. It has significant antioxidant activity and contains flavonoids, rutin, quercetin, hyperoside, triterpenoids, and rosmarinic acid, which have demonstrated anticancer properties. The plant has also shown antibacterial and antiviral activity. An anti-HIV active compound, prunellin, has been isolated from extracts of *P. vulgaris*, and extracts of the plant are reported to be effective in reducing symptoms of gingivitis.

## RECIPE

**Prunella Tea**

2–3 tablespoons fresh heal-all leaves
2 cups water

Bring water to boiling. Pour over leaves and steep for a few minutes. Strain, and sweeten with honey.

Heal-all has a long history of use.

Heal-all may increase the survival rate of people with breast cancer. In one study, patients who took heal-all along with the anticancer medication taxane lived significantly longer than those who took only the medication. The plant also prevented side effects of cancer treatment.

Heal-all is composed of native species as well as varieties introduced from Europe. The plant can be found on every continent except Antarctica. It is a popular nectar and pollen plant for many bees and butterflies.

Heal-all leaves and flower heads have beneficial properties.

Not much is known about the use of heal-all during pregnancy and nursing. To be on the safe side, avoid use or consult your health-care provider.

There are no problematic look-alike plants. Tea remains one of the most popular ways to enjoy heal-all.

Lamb's-quarter leaves are high in vitamins, minerals, and antioxidants.

# LAMB'S-QUARTER
*Chenopodium album*

**Family:** Amaranthaceae

**Also called:** Lambsquarters, bathua, baconweed, goosefoot, wild spinach, fat hen. Also called pigweed, although several different plants share this common name.

**Uses:** Leaves and tender stems, raw or cooked; seeds, processed

**Cautions:** No look-alikes. Oxalates.

**Season:** Late spring, summer

**Range:** Throughout New Jersey and Pennsylvania: gardens, fields, barnyards, disturbed areas, edges of woods; full sun, part shade

**Description:** Fast growing annual, 1'–8' tall, branched. Leaves are diamond shaped with irregular teeth, untoothed at the stem end. Mature stems are vertically grooved and may be tinged with purple, red, or shades of green. Leaves alternate up the stem; undersides have a whitish, mealy coating. Small green inconspicuous flowers are in clusters. Seeds are tiny, black.

Lamb's-quarter is one of the most nutrient-dense vegetables. This underappreciated wild plant has it all. Its mild taste is arguably better than spinach, to which it is often compared. Although considered a weed in this country, lamb's-quarter has been foraged and cultivated throughout history. Europeans valued it as a garden vegetable and brought it with them to the New World. Napoleon Bonaparte is said to have relied on lamb's-quarter seeds to feed his troops. Scientists are certain that *C. album* was gathered and used for food in prehistoric times.

Lamb's-quarter leaves sometimes have purple-tinged edges. Note the mealy white coating on emerging leaves.

Various Native American tribes ate lamb's-quarter leaves and seeds. The seeds contain 16 percent protein. They can be cooked as a grain or sprouted and eaten. Some people winnow the chaff from the seeds; others don't bother.

The leaves can be eaten in salads or cooked. Lamb's-quarter leaves provide exceptional nutrition: A 3½-ounce portion yields high levels of vitamin C (80–155 mg / 100 g), iron, manganese, vitamin A, potassium, calcium, magnesium, folate, vitamin B6, and vitamin K. They are also rich in protein, with a high proportion of essential amino acids, and have significant antioxidant activity.

Studies have revealed that lamb's-quarter possesses antiviral, antifungal, and anti-inflammatory properties. Methanolic extracts of the leaves have demonstrated activity against breast cancer, and the plant is thought to have potential against the disease.

Lamb's-quarter is very closely related to the popular grain, quinoa (*C. quinoa*) and its seeds can be used in a similar fashion. Like quinoa, lamb's-quarter seeds contain saponins, bitter soap-like compounds that can cause gastrointestinal discomfort if eaten in excess. To reduce bitterness and avoid a possible bellyache, rinse the seeds before using.

Lamb's-quarter is in the same family as spinach, beets, swiss chard, and amaranth. Like all these vegetables, the leaves contain oxalates. In large quantities, oxalates can cause kidney stones in susceptible people. Those prone to kidney stones may want to discuss with their physician before eating. Healthy people can eat lamb's-quarter in normal amounts and don't need to avoid this nutritious vegetable. Oxalates are significantly reduced by blanching, steaming, or boiling.

To positively identify lamb's-quarter, look for the uniquely shaped leaves, and a telltale mealy white coating on new growth.

Leaves can be foraged from late spring, when the plant first appears, through fall, at which time the plant may be quite tall. Older leaves do not become bitter.

Lamb's-quarter leaves are food for caterpillars, and the seeds are eaten by various bird species. The flowers are wind pollinated.

Mature lamb's-quarter stem with vertical grooves.

Mature mayapple plant with a single fruit

## MAYAPPLE
*Podophyllum peltatum*

**Family:** Berberidaceae
**Also called:** American mandrake, umbrella plant, duck's foot, ground lemon
**Uses:** Ripe fruit (without seeds), raw or cooked
**Cautions:** The plant is poisonous except for the ripe fruit (other cautions below).
**Season:** Summer
**Range:** Throughout New Jersey and Pennsylvania; rich woods, roadsides, streambanks
**Description:** Herbaceous perennial, 8"–18" tall. One or 2 leaves per plant, each leaf palmate with 5–9 lobes, coarsely notched on tips. Leaf color is green, sometimes with brownish blotches. Stem is smooth and hairless. The plant bears 1 waxy white, almost translucent flower in May. The fruit is shaped like a small lemon and completely yellow when ripe.

Mayapple is a pretty woodland plant that forms enchanting clusters of umbrellalike plants on the forest floor. Get down and peek underneath and you'll likely find a flower. Mature flowering plants have two leaves. Younger plants have one leaf and will not flower.

In May, a small green fruit will start to form. There is only one fruit to a plant. Large colonies of mayapple plants are common. By midsummer, the leaves will usually fade and die back as the fruit continues to ripen.

Ripe mayapples have a lovely fruity smell. They are quite delicious. I've never found more than a dozen or so ripe mayapples at a time. Chipmunks, squirrels, racoons, box turtles, and other woodland critters usually get to them before people do. Box turtles are important in the growth of new mayapple plants. The seeds are much more likely to germinate if they first pass through the turtle's digestive system.

If you find yourself with an abundance of mayapples, they make good jam or jelly. The only part of the plant that can be safely eaten by humans is the ripe fruit. The rest of the plant is poisonous. The seeds should be discarded, and some say the skin should also be avoided, as it can be too laxative. To be safe, consume only the flesh of the ripe mayapple. Ripe specimens are yellow with no hint of green and will come off the plant easily. The fruit should be soft to the touch and may even be a little wrinkly.

Small mayapple colony in April. Note the ramps in the background left.

Native Americans ate mayapple fruits. They also used the plant as a laxative, a treatment for warts, and to rid worms from the body. The Hurons and the Iroquois used the root to commit suicide.

Despite its deadly aspects, research has found that mayapple contains valuable medicinal substances. The plant has known antiviral activity. It is used to manufacture a resin called podophyllin, an effective drug to treat genital warts

Mayapple ripening in August. The leaves have died back.

Perfectly ripe mayapples

and plantar warts. Anticancer drugs are also manufactured from mayapple species.

Home remedies of mayapple are not advised due to risk of toxicity. Mayapple should be avoided if pregnant or nursing. Eating the fruit in large amounts is not recommended due to the laxative tendency.

In the old days, mayapple resin was the active ingredient in a famous laxative called Carter's Little Liver Pills. The formula was patented by Samuel J. Carter of Erie, Pennsylvania. Reformulated with a name change in 1959, Carter's Little Pills is still marketed, now as a laxative without the mayapple component.

Nutrient analysis of mayapple fruit is sparse. The ripe fruit is very low in fat (0.03 percent), low in protein (0.88 percent), fairly low in carbohydrates (4 percent), and is approximately 95 percent water.

If you would like to experience this unique taste of the wild, keep the precautions in mind and enjoy.

## RECIPE

**Simple Mayapple Topping**

Ripe mayapples
Honey

Cut the ripe mayapples in half. Spoon the pulp out and put through a strainer to separate out the seeds. Discard the seeds. Stir in a bit of honey if desired. A nice accompaniment to yogurt, cottage cheese, or toast.

The thin stems of mulberry are edible.

## MULBERRY
*Morus alba* and *M. rubra*

**Family:** Moraceae
**Also called:** Common mulberry
**Uses:** Ripe fruit raw, cooked, or dried; young leaves, cooked
**Cautions:** Raw leaves, green parts, and unripe fruit may be mildly toxic or hallucinogenic.
**Season:** Fruit in summer; leaves in spring
**Range:** White mulberry (*M. alba*) common throughout New Jersey and Pennsylvania; edges of fields, along roads; sun to light shade. Red mulberry (*M. rubra*) less common; an understory tree of moist woods.
**Description:** Deciduous tree. Leaves are alternate, lobed or unlobed, toothed. Fruit is an aggregate of drupelets, cylindrical. Fruit color ranges from white to dark purple-black. White mulberry has glossy leaves. Red mulberry leaves are dull, with a hairy underside.

Mulberry fruits are a tasty summertime treat. Ripe mulberries are usually dark purple and resemble blackberries. They are very juicy and squish easily. You can't pick them without staining your hands. The flavor is sweet without tartness. Mulberries were important to Native Americans, who ate the fruits fresh and dried them for storage.

Each mulberry has a very thin stem, which is edible. You don't need to pick the stems off unless you really want to spend the time.

The white, pink, red, and purple fruit of white mulberry

Chances are, if you find a mulberry tree it is likely to be the introduced *M. alba,* or white mulberry. It is much more common than the native red mulberry, *M. rubra*. Both are edible.

The common white mulberry tree can produce white, pink, red, and purple to black fruit. The fruits progress to dark purple as they ripen. Sometimes, however, they remain white on maturity and will be sweet, even though they don't look ripe.

Mulberries are rich in vitamin C.

The tree can be a weedy plant. It is considered an invasive species in Pennsylvania. It often hybridizes with our native red mulberry, threatening its genetic integrity.

White mulberry was brought from China in the late 1700s in the hopes of establishing silk production in the United States. Silkworms will only eat mulberry leaves and prefer white mulberry. The silk industry never took off, but the introduced mulberry sure did. It is now found in all Lower 48 states except for Nevada.

The pigment responsible for the deep red and purple colors of mulberries is anthocyanin. The amount increases as the fruit ripens. The pigment is associated with reduced inflammation in the body, a lower risk of heart disease, and other health benefits.

Various shapes of mulberry leaves

Mulberries are a good source of iron, and 1 cup provides more than 100 percent of the adult requirement for vitamin C.

Fruits of *M. rubra* are rich in the phenolic compounds rutin, chlorogenic acid, and gallic acid, thought to have a range of healthful properties.

The leaves are not only appreciated by silkworms. Young mulberry leaves are eaten as a vegetable in China. They contain protein, calcium, magnesium, vitamin B1, folic acid, and beta-carotene. Analysis of dried mulberry leaf powder showed significant levels of vitamin C, ranging from 100 mg to 200 mg per 100 g.

There are reports that raw leaves, green parts of the plant, and unripe fruit may be mildly toxic or hallucinogenic. So enjoy the ripe sweet berries, and cook the leaves if using.

Picturesque oxeye daisies

## OXEYE DAISY
*Leucanthemum vulgare*

**Family:** Asteraceae
**Also called:** Chrysanthemum leucanthemum, field daisy, white daisy, common daisy, moon daisy, moon penny, marguerite, dog daisy
**Uses:** Flowers, buds, and leaves; edible raw
**Cautions:** Possible allergy if sensitive to other members of the family, such as ragweed. Skin irritation in some individuals.
**Season:** Flowers June through August; leaves almost year-round
**Range:** Throughout New Jersey and Pennsylvania; roadsides, fields, pastures, disturbed areas
**Description:** Perennial herb, 2'–3' tall. Showy, daisylike flowers about 2" across with white petals surrounding a yellow center. Flowers are solitary, perched at the top of a stem. Stems are smooth to sparsely hairy, usually unbranched, arising from a basal rosette of leaves. Lower leaves are stalked, spoon shaped, and lobed or coarsely toothed. Stem leaves are smaller, alternate, and stalkless or with a short stalk.

Oxeye is the classic daisy often seen along sunny roadsides in late spring and summer. This beautiful wildflower was introduced to the United States in the nineteenth century from Europe, where it was cultivated in gardens and used in traditional herbal medicine. It escaped cultivation and is now found in all fifty states. Oxeye daisy is a charming wildflower, an edible plant, and a plentiful weed.

Lower leaves of oxeye daisy

Oxeye daisy leaves are good to eat, especially if picked before flowering occurs. Older leaves can be somewhat bitter and may be better cooked. A good crop of leaves can even be found in winter. They are tasty eaten raw as salad greens.

The leaves are rich in vitamin A. Leaves collected in late winter and early spring were shown to contain from 7,000 to 12,000 units of vitamin A per 100 g (3½-ounce) sample. A 2-ounce serving of oxeye daisy leaves provides the full

RECIPE

**Oxeye Herb Dip**

¾ cup sour cream
½ cup mayonnaise
2–3 scallions, white and green parts, chopped fine
¼ cup finely chopped oxeye daisy leaves
1 tablespoon chopped fresh dill (or 1 teaspoon dried)
2 tablespoons chopped fresh parsley
Salt and pepper to taste

In a medium bowl, combine the sour cream, mayonnaise, scallions, oxeye daisy leaves, and herbs. Mix well; season to taste with salt and pepper. Chill for at least 1 hour. Serve with crackers, bread, or fresh veggies.

daily dietary allowance of vitamin A. In addition, the vitamin C content is significant (23 mg per 3½-ounce serving), about the same as fresh tomatoes.

The flowers have been used to make wine. Fresh daisies are lovely when used to decorate cakes. They can also be batter-dipped and made into fritters. Oxeye flowers are mild tasting to slightly peppery. The white petals are a nice addition to a green salad; an entire flower makes a pretty garnish, although it may not be palatable eaten whole. Oxeye daisy root can also be eaten, raw or cooked.

Folk medicine uses of the plant are many. Oxeye daisy has been used as a diuretic, a skin salve, and a treat-

Oxeye daisy, a composite flower

ment for asthma, whooping cough, and other respiratory ills. The plant has antioxidant and antimicrobial properties that may be responsible for some of the reported medicinal applications.

The bright blooms of oxeye daisies are easy to see on a moonlit night, hence the common names moon daisy and moon penny. It is often confused with the Shasta daisy, a popular garden flower and "look-alike" that is also safe to eat. The Shasta daisy was created in late 1800s by American botanist Luther Burbank by crossbreeding oxeye daisy with other wild European and Japanese daisies. The resultant horticultural success, Shasta daisy, has larger showier flowers and a longer bloom time compared to its wild ancestor.

Oxeye daisies are a source of pollen and nectar for a variety of visitors, including ants, bees, wasps, moths, and butterflies.

Tiny purslane flowers open in the morning.

## PURSLANE
*Portulaca oleracea*

**Family:** Portulacaceae
**Also called:** Pusley, verdolaga, little hogweed
**Uses:** Aboveground parts, raw or cooked
**Cautions:** Oxalates, look-alike plants
**Season:** Late spring through summer
**Range:** Throughout New Jersey and Pennsylvania; sunny, moist locations
**Description:** A sprawling succulent, grows in a mat-like form. Individual stems up to 18" long. Leaves are glossy green, paddle-shaped, up to about 1" long. Stems are smooth, round, usually reddish (green in younger plants). Flowers are yellow, tiny, about ¼" across. They close at night and open in the morning. Flower forms a tiny seed capsule filled with black seeds.

A while back, I came to the realization that this summer weed in my vegetable garden was really a volunteer crop. And the nutritionist in me was blown away when I discovered that wild purslane is more nutritious that most of the vegetables I have been growing on purpose.

Declared by some to be one of the world's worst agricultural weeds, purslane has a nutrient profile that puts most cultivated vegetables to shame. It contains huge amounts of alpha-linolenic acid (ALA), one of the omega-3 fatty acids, or "good" fats that most of us need more of. In fact, purslane has more ALA than any other green leafy vegetable on the planet.

**Purslane Panzanella**

¼ cup olive oil

2 tablespoons balsamic vinegar

1½ cups purslane tips and leaves

1 cucumber, peeled and diced

4 ripe tomatoes, cut in chunks

¼ cup thinly sliced red onion

¼ cup torn basil leaves

4 ounces mozzarella cheese, in bite-size pieces

4 cups stale Italian bread or rolls, in bite-size chunks

In a large bowl, whisk together the oil and vinegar. Add the purslane, cucumber, tomatoes, onion, basil, and mozzarella. Toss to combine. Add the bread. Let stand for 15 minutes before serving.

Why does this matter? ALA is essential to human health. There is evidence that eating foods high in this omega-3 fat can reduce high blood pressure and help prevent cardiovascular disease and heart attacks. Wild purslane also boasts high concentrations of potassium, magnesium, calcium, vitamin C, and beta-carotene.

Purslane has a nice crisp juiciness to it. The flavor is faintly lemony, another plus. As for the mouthfeel, I like to use the word "mucilaginous." There are

some who find this quality a bit off-putting and might even describe purslane as slimy. I don't find the texture objectionable. The mucilaginous quality makes purslane suitable for soups and stews, lending a slight thickening quality.

Preparation is simple. Snip stems near the base of the plant, give them a rinse, and chop. You can then toss them into a soup,

Reddish stems of purslane

Freshly harvested purslane stems

Note the purslane on top, spurge on the bottom. Spurge is toxic.

sauté like spinach, or use fresh in salads or smoothies. Mixed into scrambled eggs, purslane becomes a nutritious dish that doesn't even require a recipe.

The plant's native status is uncertain. Although it is generally accepted that settlers brought it with them from Europe, there is also evidence that Native Americans were eating purslane before Europeans arrived.

Purslane contains high amounts of oxalates, as do many other foods. Oxalates can cause kidney stones in susceptible people. If your doctor has told you not to eat too much spinach or other high-oxalate foods, purslane would be on that list of vegetables. Most of us don't need to worry about moderate consumption of such otherwise nutritious foods.

A plant called spurge (*Chamaesyce* spp.) may be considered a look-alike. Spurge is toxic. While they don't look all that similar, I have witnessed people having difficulty telling the two apart. Purslane leaves are fleshy or succulent. Spurge is not succulent. The stem of spurge exudes a milky white sap when broken (this sap is an irritant). The sap of purslane, if any, will be clear. They sometimes grow together.

Queen Anne's lace, or wild carrot, is often seen as a weed.

## QUEEN ANNE'S LACE / WILD CARROT
*Daucus carota*

**Family:** Apiaceae

**Also called:** Bird's nest, bishop's lace

**Uses:** All parts edible, raw or cooked

**Cautions:** Do not use if pregnant or nursing. The sap may cause skin irritation in some. Poisonous look-alike species.

**Season:** Year-round

**Range:** Throughout New Jersey and Pennsylvania; dry fields, roadsides, waste areas

**Description:** Biennial, 2'–3' in height. Stem is green and covered with short, coarse hairs. Leaves are finely divided, with a lacy appearance; leaf undersides are hairy. Flat-topped clusters of tiny white flowers, each with 5 petals. Cluster often has a dark red or purple flower in the center. Delicate 3-pronged bracts at the base of each flower. Mature flower curls up into a bird's nest shape. Taproot is whitish. Leaves, stems, and root have a definite carroty smell.

Queen Anne's lace, or wild carrot, is native to Europe and Asia. It is the ancestor of the bright orange root vegetable we all know as a carrot. Although wild carrot is white rooted and cultivated carrots are orange, the two are essentially the same plant. Selective breeding of the wild variety has produced a larger and sweeter vegetable.

Queen Anne's lace foliage

Wild carrot was introduced to North America in the seventeenth century. It's been recognized as food and medicine since ancient times. Ecologists tend to view it as a weed.

Wild carrot displays carrot-like foliage in its first year and flowers in its second year. To harvest the root, pull it up in the first year, or in the second year before flowering occurs. The thin, pale root has a definite carrot smell and flavor. When mature, it becomes less palatable, but the woody core is easily removed after cooking. Older roots or entire plants can be simmered to make vegetable broth.

The fresh leaves of wild carrot have a pronounced flavor and are commonly consumed in Mediterranean countries. They are eaten raw or added to cooked dishes. The lacy flower makes a decorative edible garnish on any dish. Wild carrot seeds are tasty when used as a seasoning and added to soups, etc. They are abundant and easy to gather.

Upper left, the bird's nest shape of a mature Queen Anne's lace seed head

Unlike most wild foods, wild carrot is less nutritious than its cultivated counterpart. The wild carrot root lacks the orange coloring

The hairy stems of Queen Anne's lace

(beta-carotene) that was bred into market carrots. But the wild version still has value. The leaves are rich in apigenin and luteolin, compounds that demonstrate antioxidant and anti-inflammatory properties. Extracts of the seeds show anti-oxidant and antibacterial activity.

Native Americans used the plant as food, as a diuretic, as a skin wash, and more. Throughout European history, the seeds of Queen Anne's lace have been employed as a contraceptive. This traditional use, dating back more than 2,000 years to when Hippocrates described use of wild carrot seed for birth control, is continued by modern-day herbalists. Lab studies on animals show *D. carota* to have an antifertility effect, but there is inadequate information regarding efficacy and safety in humans. Until more is known, wild carrot seed should not be used during pregnancy, or relied upon for contraceptive use.

## RECIPE

**Wild Carrot Seeds (for spice or tea)**

Snip the dried seed heads into a container or a paper bag. When agitated, the seeds will separate out. Winnow away the chaff in a light breeze. Grind the seeds in a spice grinder or coffee grinder or with a mortar and pestle. Use small amounts as a spice in cooked dishes. The seed can also be brewed into tea. Use about 1 teaspoon per cupful of boiling water, and steep for 3–5 minutes. Sweeten as desired.

The flower cluster of Queen Anne's lace will often have a dark spot in the middle.

When foraging, we always need to be aware of possible look-alike plants in order to be safe. This is especially important with wild carrot. The deadly poisonous hemlock plant (*Conium maculatum*) looks similar. If you are not 100 percent sure that your plant is wild carrot, do not harvest it.

One important identifying characteristic is a hairy stem. The green stem of wild carrot is always covered with short, coarse hairs. The leaf undersides are hairy as well. Poison hemlock is hairless and has purple spots or markings on the stems.

To summarize, your plant should have no purple spots, blotches, or markings on the stem, and the stem should be hairy. It may help to remember this oft-repeated adage: "The Queen has hairy legs." Wild carrot, especially the root, will smell like carrot.

Black swallowtail caterpillars feed on the leaves of Queen Anne's lace. The dark flower often present in the center of the flower head is said to represent a drop of blood from when Queen Anne pricked her finger while making lace. Botanists believe the purplish flower serves to attract insects.

Ripe serviceberry with characteristic five-pointed calyx.

## SERVICEBERRY
*Amelanchier* spp.

**Family:** Rosaceae

**Also called:** Juneberry, saskatoon berry, shadberry, shadblow

**Uses:** Fruit, raw or cooked

**Cautions:** None

**Season:** Late spring

**Range:** Throughout New Jersey and Pennsylvania; woods, roadsides, thickets; sun to part shade

**Description:** Shrub or a small tree under 40'. Leaves are alternate, oval, 2"–4" long, finely toothed. Flowers are white, 5-petaled, in loose, drooping terminal clusters. The fruit is dark red to purple-black when ripe, about ⅓" diameter, with a 5-pointed "crown" at one end. The bark is grayish and smooth, and the plant is thornless.

Serviceberry, also called Juneberry for the month in which the berries ripen, is a delicious wild fruit. Serviceberries are chewy, juicy, and arguably better tasting than blueberries, which they resemble. Both fruits bear a five-pointed calyx, or crown, the remnants of the original flower.

Serviceberry blooms before most other shrubs or trees, and its white flowers are easily seen in the still-leafless woodlands. This provides a good way to locate the plant for future foraging.

Serviceberry is one of the first wild fruits to ripen. The berries are purple-black at maturity, but I find them perfectly delicious when dark red. They are great made into pies, jam, and muffins—pretty much anywhere you would use blueberries. There are ten seeds to a berry. Serviceberry seeds are soft and lend a taste of almond to the toothsome fruit.

Although the plants are native in the wild, you may be more likely to find them as planted specimens. Serviceberry is frequently grown as a landscape plant, primarily as an ornamental.

Serviceberry was an important food source of indigenous peoples. The berries were eaten fresh or dried for winter use. They were a main ingredient in pemmican. The fruit was used for upset stomach, as a laxative, and as eye and ear medicine. The wood and twigs were used for baskets, arrows, pipe stems, and tool handles.

Serviceberry fruits are an excellent source of the minerals iron, magnesium, and manganese and are rich in protein, fat, calcium, potassium, copper, and carotenoids such as lutein.

The vitamin C content of the berries (104–122 mg / 100 g) is higher than that of most common fruits, including kiwi, orange, and strawberry. A 3½-ounce serving of ripe serviceberries provides more than 100 percent of the recommended daily intake of vitamin C.

Serviceberries are also rich in anthocyanins, which are largely responsible for the antioxidant properties of the fruit, and this increases with ripening. The berries also contain the beneficial compounds chlorogenic acid, catechins, and rutin.

Serviceberries freeze well, and the anthocyanins are known to be very well preserved in the frozen state.

Serviceberry trees planted on a college campus

It can be difficult to tell *Amelanchier* species apart, since they may appear similar and hybridize readily. Common in the area are downy serviceberry (*A. arborea*) and smooth serviceberry (*A. laevis*). These species are often crossbred to produce cultivars for landscaping. Shadblow serviceberry (*A. canadensis*) is also commonly used in the trade.

In colonial times, the blooming of the plant indicated that the ground had thawed sufficiently to conduct burial services for those who had died during the winter, hence the name serviceberry. The name shadbush comes from the tree's blooming when the shad migrate upriver to spawn.

Serviceberries are important food for wildlife and are eagerly eaten by birds.

Spearmint has opposite, sharply-toothed leaves and a distinct smell.

# SPEARMINT
*Mentha spicata*

**Family:** Lamiaceae
**Also called:** Garden mint, common mint, lamb mint, green mint
**Uses:** Leaves in beverages, cooked dishes
**Cautions:** Gastroesophageal reflux disease (GERD), pregnancy, nursing (see below).
**Season:** Spring through fall
**Range:** Throughout New Jersey and Pennsylvania; moist rich soil, streambanks, ditches; full sun to part shade
**Description:** Perennial herb up to 2' tall. Square stem. Leaves opposite, sharply toothed, aromatic with strong smell of spearmint when crushed. Leaf stalk very short or absent. Flowers light pink to light purple in slender spikes, both terminal and from leaf axils. Blooms in mid- to late summer.

Spearmint has a long history of use as an aromatic flavoring. Native to Europe, the plant was brought to North America by colonists for culinary and medicinal uses. The minty leaves have a refreshing flavor, and the plant is commonly used for digestive problems.

There are many species of mint, and they all have a definite minty aroma. The two most common are peppermint and spearmint. It can be hard to tell the various species apart. Even botanists find it difficult, since mints hybridize with one another.

**Peas with Spearmint**

2 tablespoons butter
12 ounces peas (fresh or frozen)
2 tablespoons finely chopped spearmint leaves
Salt and pepper

In a large skillet, melt the butter over medium. Add the peas and cook, stirring occasionally, until the peas are heated through. Stir in the spearmint. Add salt and pepper to taste.

Spearmint is named for its spear-shaped leaves. Its flavor is frequently incorporated into toothpaste, chewing gum, and candy, although most manufacturers use synthetic flavoring nowadays.

The flavor of the spearmint plant is more subtle than that of peppermint (*M. piperita*), which has a sharp menthol taste. Peppermint is a hybrid of watermint (*M. aquatica*) and spearmint.

A rule of thumb: If a plant looks like a mint with a square stem and opposite leaves and smells minty, you can safely assume it is a mint.

A refreshing herbal tea can be made by steeping the leaves in hot water for a few minutes (the longer the stronger). Enjoy hot or chilled. In the Middle East, Moroccan mint tea is very popular. It is made from green tea, spearmint leaves, and sugar.

Spearmint's mellow flavor complements both sweet and savory dishes. It works well in fruit salads. Steamed or roasted veggies are good topped with the minced leaves. Lemonade benefits from spearmint. And then there's always the mint mojito, a classic cocktail made by steeping muddled (crushed) mint leaves in sugar and rum.

The flavor of spearmint is said to be better before the plant flowers, but I have not noticed a difference. Mint leaves can be dried for year-round use.

Fresh spearmint leaves are rich in iron, vitamin C, vitamin A, folate, manganese, magnesium, and potassium, and are high in protein (18 percent by weight). A mere 2-tablespoon serving (11 g) of spearmint provides 9 percent of the daily value for iron and vitamin A. The leaves also contain the beneficial gamma-tocopherol form of vitamin E.

*M. spicata* is used worldwide in traditional medicine for cold, cough, fever, indigestion, vomiting, cramps, and insomnia. Studies show it to be analgesic, anti-inflammatory, antimicrobial, antispasmodic, and antipyretic. This supports

Spearmint, like all mints, has a square stem.

some uses of spearmint in folk medicine. It is rich in rosmarinic acid, a potent antioxidant, and other beneficial compounds. The plant's distinctive smell and flavor are from a chemical called carvone.

Research suggests that spearmint tea may be effective when used as a treatment for hirsutism in women. The tea is commonly used by women in Middle Eastern countries as a treatment for the condition.

The spearmint plant is generally considered safe in normal dietary amounts. You may want to avoid it, however, if you have issues with heartburn. Mint of any kind can trigger GERD (aka acid reflux or heartburn). Although mint calms and soothes the digestive tract, it also relaxes the sphincter at the top of the stomach, which can permit stomach juices to back up into the esophagus.

The safety of wild mint during pregnancy and nursing is unknown. To be safe, avoid use. Oil of mint, commercially extracted, can be toxic, so caution is advised. It is much more concentrated than the natural plant.

If you wish to grow your own spearmint, know that all mints spread quickly and can be invasive. Grow in a pot to keep it contained.

*Fragaria virginiana* with hairy stems and a nibbled fruit

## STRAWBERRY / WILD STRAWBERRY
*Fragaria virginiana*

**Family:** Rosaceae

**Also called:** Virginia strawberry, common strawberry

**Uses:** Fruit eaten fresh or cooked into jam, desserts; leaves made into tea

**Cautions:** Avoid with strawberry allergy.

**Season:** Spring, summer

**Range:** Throughout New Jersey and Pennsylvania; fields, meadows, recently disturbed area, woodland edges, openings in woods

**Description:** Low ground-hugging perennial. Leaves are on long hairy petioles and consist of 3 leaflets, coarsely toothed. The end tooth of the middle leaflet is usually smaller than the 2 adjacent teeth. Flowers are white with 5 petals. Flower stalks are hairy. Fruit usually less than ½" across, red when ripe. Seeds are sunken into surface of the flesh. Plant spreads by runners, which root to form new plants.

The delectable fruit of wild *Fragaria virginiana* is much smaller than a commercial strawberry, but the flavor of this native species is considered far superior. Wild strawberries are usually eaten raw, but if collected in sufficient quantity can be made into jams, cobblers, shortcakes, or any number of desserts. The dried leaves make a flavorful and nourishing tea.

Strawberry leaves and fruit are rich in vitamin C. The fruit shows high antioxidant activity, and analysis of the ascorbic acid (vitamin C) content of wild strawberries is shown to be approximately equal to that of oranges.

Typical wild strawberry leaves, white flower

The fruit was relished by Native Americans. The Lenape called it heart berry. The Cherokee held wild strawberry in the mouth to remove dental tartar. The plant was used for diarrhea, kidney problems, and jaundice. It was taken for scurvy, effective due to the vitamin C content.

Supermarket strawberries are a cross between our native wild strawberry and the South American strawberry *F. chiloensis* which is a much larger fruit.

Wild strawberry is pollinated by a wide variety of bees, flies, and ants. It usually reproduces by stolons (runners), which are long stems sent out along the ground by the mother plant to produce new plants. Wild strawberry occasionally reproduces by seed as well.

A similar species, wood strawberry (*F. vesca*) is less commonly found. It has smaller fruits that are generally considered less tasty than *F. virginiana*.

Mock strawberry (*Potentilla indica*) is far more common than either of the wild strawberry species. Mock strawberry, common in lawns, is a tasteless imposter. Also known as Indian strawberry since it is native to India, it is not a true strawberry.

Wood strawberry leaves and flower

Mock strawberry, a nutritious but tasteless look-alike

But it does fool a lot of people, who believe they have tiny tasteless strawberries growing in their yard.

The mock variety has yellow flowers. The tiny fruits are red and have small seeds on the surface. Although perfectly edible, they have very little flavor. A participant in one of my foraging programs described it perfectly when she said it was "like eating crunchy water."

Mock strawberry leaves are a good source of vitamin C, measuring at 79 mg per 100 g. The leaves are mild tasting and are available almost year-round for tea. The fruit possesses anti-inflammatory properties.

RECIPE

**Wild Strawberries and Homemade Whipped Cream**

1 cup heavy cream
½ cup powdered sugar
2 cups wild strawberries, halved if desired
A few strawberries for garnish

Use an electric mixer on medium to high speed and whip the cream until thickened and a little fluffy. Add the powdered sugar. Continue to beat on low speed until combined, then on high speed until stiff peaks form and it looks like whipped cream. Layer the berries and whipped cream in small dishes or parfait glasses. Garnish with a perfect little strawberry.

Watercress pulled from a stream. Note the white roots.

## WATERCRESS
*Nasturtium officinale*

**Family:** Brassicaceae
**Also called:** Rorippa nasturtium, water rocket, yellowcress
**Uses:** Leaves, raw or cooked
**Cautions:** Cleanliness of location
**Season:** Year-round
**Range:** Throughout New Jersey and Pennsylvania; cool, slow-moving water: springs, brooks, streams, ditches
**Description:** Trailing aquatic plant. Starts as small rosette. Stems grow to 2'–3' long and are hollow, with roots that form at nodes. Leaves are pinnately compound, 3–9 leaflets; terminal leaflet is larger. Leaflets are roughly oval shaped. Small, white 4-petaled flowers appear in summer.

Watercress is one of the most nutritious wild foods, and officially a powerhouse vegetable. The peppery tasting leafy veggie is ranked number one on the list of "Powerhouse Fruits and Vegetables" published by the US Centers for Disease

Control in 2014. Foods on the list are those most strongly associated with a reduction of chronic disease risk.

While this is just one of many food classification systems, it does reinforce the fact that watercress is an exceptionally healthful, nutrient-dense food. It is high in vitamins A (beta-carotene), C, and K, the B vitamins, potassium, manganese, and many other nutrients. The nutritional superiority of watercress is not surprising since it is in the mustard family. Also known as the cruciferous vegetables, this group includes kale, collards, and cauliflower.

Watercress is one of the oldest known leafy vegetables eaten by humans. It has been used since ancient times for an array of conditions, including cancer, diabetes, and tuberculosis, and as a diuretic. It was brought to North America by European settlers as a food plant valued it for its ability to treat and prevent scurvy (a vitamin C–deficiency disease).

Watercress is an excellent source of antioxidants, including quercetin and kaempferol. It is also very rich in carotenoids, which are protective against cancer, heart disease, and age-related

A colony of watercress in a stream

Watercress flowers are fine to eat.

eye disease. The high concentration of vitamin K and bone-protecting minerals in watercress may help ward off osteoporosis.

You will find the plant growing in slow-moving shallow water, where it tends to form large tangled mats. Be careful about water quality. To avoid pollutants, don't harvest near agricultural or industrial sites. Watercress may also harbor organisms like liver flukes, which can make you ill. It's not always easy to tell how clean a water source is. If you're lucky enough to have access to a spring where the plant grows safe from contaminants, then enjoy your watercress in a salad. Otherwise cook it. It will mellow the pungent taste and kill any organisms that may be present.

Watercress soup is a great way to use the plant. This simple recipe was enjoyed at an invasive plants workshop at the Deserted Village of Feltville in Berkeley Heights, New Jersey. Participants were encouraged to pull the plant from a pond where it was taking over. Watercress, a non-native species, can become pretty invasive in some water bodies.

To harvest the plant, clip only the leaves that grow above the water's surface. Wash well in cold water, then incorporate into any recipe where you would use cooked greens such as spinach.

Watercress can even be found growing in winter. I have seen it looking fresh and bright green while partially covered in snow.

Ducks and muskrats eat the leaves of watercress. The flowers are pollinated by bees and flies.

Wood sorrel with heart-shaped leaflets and yellow flower; purslane in the foreground

## WOOD SORREL
*Oxalis stricta*

**Family:** Oxalidaeae
**Also called:** Oxalis, sourgrass, sour clover, yellow wood sorrel
**Uses:** Aboveground parts, raw or cooked
**Cautions:** Oxalic acid (see below)
**Season:** Spring through early fall
**Range:** Throughout New Jersey and Pennsylvania; lawns, flowerbeds, disturbed areas, fields, woodlands; sun to part shade
**Description:** Upright or sprawling plant, up to 8" tall. Leaves on long petioles, palmately compound with 3 heart-shaped leaflets. Each leaflet creased down the middle; edges are untoothed. Flowers are yellow, 5-petaled, about ½" across, and bloom spring through summer. Fruits are upright green seedpods, up to 1" long, on a sharp angle from the stem.

Wood sorrel is a cute little plant. With its perfect heart-shaped leaflets and delicate yellow flowers, it is easy to identify. Each heart has a crease in the middle that allows it to close up, which it does at night. It opens again in the morning but will close again in bright sun or rain.

Another remarkable feature of wood sorrel is its taste. I love to watch people who are experiencing it for the first time. They are invariably surprised, and usually delighted, by its bright lemony flavor. The plant is famous for its tart taste and is named accordingly. "Sorrel" derives from a French word meaning "sour," and "oxalis" comes from the Greek *oxus*, which also means "sour."

Lemony wood sorrel seedpods

Indigenous people chewed the plant to alleviate thirst. They also utilized it for fever, nausea, and as a mouthwash.

The leaves, flowers, seedpods, and tender stems are all good to eat. Wood sorrel is a great trailside nibble. The little upright seedpods look like tiny okra pods. They deliver quite a lemony burst.

Wood sorrel adds a refreshing acid component to salads. The plant also makes a nice cold beverage. Steep for 5–10 minutes in hot water. You can drink it at this point or chill it and enjoy a glass of tangy, refreshing iced wood sorrel tea. Sweeten as you please.

Analysis of *O. stricta* reveals a high vitamin C content, 47–58 mg per 100 g (3½ ounces), as well as 106 mg of calcium and 7 mg of iron per serving. It is very low in calories.

Even though it is a nutritious food, wood sorrel should not be eaten in huge quantities. It is relatively high in oxalic acid, which can inhibit calcium absorption. Many nutritious foods, including almonds, spinach, and sweet potatoes, are high in oxalic acid. For most of us, wood sorrel is fine eaten in normal amounts. Enjoy its flavor in salads or smoothies, nibble it from your garden, and add it to cooked dishes. That said, if your health-care provider has advised you to limit high-oxalate foods such as spinach, put wood sorrel on that list.

Wood sorrel is sometimes misidentified as clover (*Trifolium* spp.), another edible weed of gardens. Clover has rounded leaflets, not heart-shaped.

Sheep sorrel (*Rumex acetosella*), also known as sour weed, is another tart wild green. Although unrelated, the plants share the sorrel name and have a similar lemony flavor. They can be used in the same way and have similar cautions due to oxalic acid content. The leaves of sheep sorrel have an elongated arrowhead-shape.

Wood sorrel is pollinated by bees, ants, and butterflies. It is plentiful in the area, and there are no concerns at this time regarding overharvesting.

Sheep sorrel has arrowhead-shaped leaves and tastes like wood sorrel.

# Plants of Fall

Clusters of autumn olive berries

## AUTUMN OLIVE
*Elaeagnus umbellata*

**Family:** Elaeagnaceae
**Also called:** Japanese silverberry, silverberry, autumnberry
**Uses:** Berries, raw or cooked
**Cautions:** Contaminated areas
**Season:** Late summer to fall
**Range:** Throughout New Jersey and Pennsylvania; disturbed areas, thickets, meadows, roadsides, forest openings; full sun to part shade
**Description:** Deciduous shrub or small spreading tree up to 15' high. Leaves are alternate, simple, oval to lance-shaped leaves, 2"–3" long. They are green above and covered with silvery scales below. Leaf with wavy margins, smooth or wavy, no teeth. Flowers appear in spring. They are small, creamy white or pale yellow, and very fragrant. Fruit is red, juicy, flecked with silvery speckles, less than ½" in diameter with a single seed. Some branches develop thorns.

Although it has become an ecologist's nightmare, autumn olive is one of the "best kept secrets" of the foraging world. Not at all related to the brackish olives

Autumn olive berries are tasty and nutritious.

we enjoy in salads, autumn olive berries are sweet-tart and juicy. They are bright red with silver speckles that sparkle in the sun. Each has a single soft seed inside; you can eat it or spit it out.

The berries are astringent and unappealing if underripe, but when fully mature in late summer and fall, autumn olive berries become quite delicious. They are sweet, balanced with a bit of tartness. They can be enjoyed straight from the bush or made into delicious jam, jelly, sauce, or fruit leather. Autumn olive is a great late-season foraging plant. Harvest time is September, well into fall.

The red color of autumn olive berries comes from lycopene, a powerful anti-oxidant believed to protect against heart disease and various types of cancer.

## RECIPE

**Autumn Olive Sauce**

Collect about 4 cups of ripe autumn olive berries. Rinse them and put them in a large saucepan with just enough water to keep them from burning, about ½ cup. Cover and cook gently, mashing the fruit in the pot and giving an occasional stir. When the juices are released, let cool somewhat and then strain the seeds out. A sieve, strainer, or a food mill works for this. Add sugar or other sweetener to taste. The sauce is delicious on pancakes or waffles. Swirl it into yogurt or add to your favorite smoothie for a super antioxidant boost. Keep refrigerated and use within a week or two. **Note:** The more sugar, the longer it keeps.

Tomatoes are considered a rich source, and autumn olives have a much higher concentration. As with most fruits, the darker the better, for flavor as well as nutritional value.

Autumn olive berries contain 91 calories and 28 mg of vitamin C in a 3½-ounce portion, as well as significant amounts of calcium, zinc, iron, manganese, and magnesium. The fruit is also rich in carotenoids, which are known

Silvery undersides of autumn olive leaves

to have strong anticancer and anti-inflammatory properties. The exceptional lycopene content, along with other nutrients and antioxidants, makes autumn olive one of our most nutritious wild fruits.

Native to eastern Asia, autumn olive was introduced into the United States in 1830 for use in strip mine reclamation, erosion control, and as an ornamental shrub. It has since become one of the most problematic invasive plants in the eastern United States. It does well in poor soil and quickly takes over natural areas. Birds eat the fruit and facilitate its spread. So harvest all you want. Just don't scatter the seeds where they might sprout.

The closely related Russian olive (*E. angustifolia*) is a look-alike plant. Its fruit is gray-green or yellowish and is edible although mealy. Russian olive is also invasive but is less common than autumn olive in the area.

Be careful of autumn olive growing in contaminated areas such as old strip mine sites, where toxic levels of heavy metals can wind up in the fruit.

The distinctly silvery undersides of autumn olive leaves make this shrub easy to spot along roadsides, where it grows abundantly. The berries are eaten by a variety of wildlife, and the flowers are pollinated by insects.

The beautiful bark of American beech

## BEECH
*Fagus grandifolia*

**Family:** Fagaceae
**Also called:** American beech, beechnut tree
**Uses:** Young leaves edible, raw or cooked; nutmeats cooked, small quantities when raw
**Cautions:** Nuts in excess (see below)
**Season:** Spring leaves; nuts in fall
**Range:** Throughout New Jersey and Pennsylvania, less abundant in southern Pennsylvania; shaded woodlands or sunny open sites
**Description:** Deciduous tree, 50'–80'; may grow taller. Twigs are slender and zigzag. Leaf buds about 1" long and pointed, with a thornlike appearance. Leaves are alternate, simple, elliptical, 2½"–5" long, with parallel veins. Leaf tips are pointed; edges are sharply serrated. Flowers inconspicuous. Fruit consists of a spiny 4-lobed husk, about ¾" long, with 2 (sometimes 3) nuts inside. Each nut (the "beechnut") is triangular and shiny brown. Seeds ripen in fall. Tree bark is thin, smooth, and light gray or silver gray.

Our native American beech is a large, elegant, slow-growing tree with strikingly smooth gray bark. This smoothness is why beech is the tree you're most likely to see carved with hearts and initials. This practice mars the beauty of the tree and leaves it susceptible to infection.

Beech tree seeds, commonly known as beechnuts, have long been used as food by humans. The nuts are small but tasty. Like most edible seeds and nuts, beechnuts are a concentrated source of nutrients. Analysis of dried beechnuts shows they are rich in potassium, copper, manganese, and the B vitamins,

Tender beech leaves of early spring are mild tasting.

especially folate and B6. A 1-ounce portion has 161 calories and 1.7 g of protein. Calcium, vitamin C, and iron are also present in significant amounts.

Native Americans ate the nuts and young beech foliage. Beechnuts were cooked in a variety of ways. The leaves were eaten and used medicinally, often for skin conditions. Cherokee chewed beechnuts as an anthelmintic (for worms). They used beech wood for lumber and to make buttons. Early settlers ate beechnuts and extracted the nut oil for food use and lamp oil. The inner bark was dried and ground into flour.

Tender young beech leaves are good raw or cooked as greens. They blend nicely into a mixed spring salad. This recipe celebrates the various tender greens of April and May.

Beechnuts can be foraged from the ground among fallen autumn leaves or from lower tree branches. You may find nuts that have fallen out of their bristly husks. These are fine to collect; just check for insect holes.

Collecting the kernels in quantity sufficient to use in a recipe may be difficult. The outer husk is easily removed, but extracting the little nuggets from their shells is a fiddly task. The shiny, leathery shells can be peeled away with your thumbnail. Some nuts may be empty or have unformed kernels.

Beechnuts contain saponin glycosides, which can cause gastric upset. The substance is deactivated by heat, and cooking the nuts makes them taste better and easier to digest. They can be oven-roasted for 5–10 minutes until crisp and fragrant.

Fallen beechnuts with open husks

Shiny triangular-shaped beechnut shells

Beech trees often retain their pale, dry leaves through winter. This feature makes for a ghostly appearance in snowy woods and provides an additional way to identify beech.

Beech wood makes excellent lumber and is used for veneer, flooring, furniture, cabinets, and musical instruments.

Bears, foxes, deer, porcupines, rabbits, squirrels, turkeys, blue jays, and other woodland creatures eat beechnuts or store them away in the fall.

Black walnuts drop from the tree when ripe.

## BLACK WALNUT
*Juglans nigra*

**Family:** Juglandaceae
**Also called:** American walnut
**Uses:** Nuts, eaten or pressed for oil
**Cautions:** Those with nut allergy should avoid.
**Season:** Fall
**Range:** Throughout New Jersey and Pennsylvania
**Description:** Deciduous tree, up to 130'. Leaves alternate, pinnately compound, 1'–2' long. Each has 11–23 finely serrated leaflets, terminal leaflet small or absent. Fruit is spherical, 2"–3" across, consisting of 3 layers: fleshy outer husk (hull), hard corrugated shell, and nut-meat. Husk is green, ripens to yellowish.

Black walnuts are our native walnuts. They are stronger tasting than the more commercially successful English walnuts we're used to seeing in supermarkets. While the English variety is cultivated for its mild-flavored nutmeats, black walnut is grown mainly for its wood. But many people relish the earthy flavor of black walnut.

Found throughout eastern North America, black walnut was an important food source for native peoples for centuries. The nutmeats were often added to pemmican and other traditional dishes.

Research verifies the nutritional excellence of black walnuts. They possess an impressive array of vitamins and minerals and are richer in protein than English walnuts. They contain compounds that promote heart health and exhibit anti-cancer properties. Black walnuts are especially rich in omega-3 fatty acids, the "good" fats. They are low in carbohydrates and high in magnesium, potassium, iron, zinc, copper, manganese, and selenium.

Black walnut has been long been used to treat a variety of ills, including intestinal worms, syphilis, various infections, and skin conditions. Native American tribes used the green husks for many ailments and made a tonic from the bark to treat rheumatism. Research supporting medicinal uses is limited.

Black walnuts ripen in the fall and will drop from the tree when ripe. You can forage them off the ground or pick them from the tree if they're ripe enough. The hull will give a little when pressed with a finger. Underripe ones are very solid. The fruits have an odd scent that I enjoy, kind of lemony-medicinal. Ripe husks are yellow and may have some dark spots.

The husk needs to be removed. If it remains on the nut for too long, juice will seep into the nut meat and make it taste bad. Don a pair of rubber gloves for this part. The dark goop in the husk will stain your hands for a week—voice of experience here. Put on some old shoes or boots, and stomp and roll the nuts underfoot. Rinse to remove most of the mushy debris off the shells.

You could crack and eat the nuts now, but if you dry them for a couple of weeks, you'll be rewarded with better flavor. To dry, lay them out in a single layer on screens or some newspaper in a well-ventilated area, away from squirrels. A shed, garage, or dry basement is perfect.

Ripe husks are yellowish and may have some dark spots.

Black walnut is one tough nut to crack.

Now the toughest part: getting to the nutmeat inside. English walnuts have a thin shell compared to black walnuts. I find it amazing that squirrels have such an easy time chewing through black walnuts.

### RECIPE

**Wild Walnut Granola**

2 cups old-fashioned oats
1 cup walnut pieces
½ cup sunflower seeds
1 teaspoon cinnamon
¼ teaspoon salt
¼ cup vegetable oil
¼ cup honey or maple syrup
1 teaspoon vanilla extract
½ cup raisins or dried cranberries

Preheat oven to 350°F. Line a baking sheet with parchment paper. In a mixing bowl, combine the oats, walnuts, seeds, cinnamon, and salt. Do not add the raisins yet. Stir in the oil, sweetener, and vanilla. Mix well. Spread onto the baking sheet. Bake for 20–25 minutes, stirring halfway through. When done, granola should be lightly golden. Remove from oven and add the raisins. Cool and store in an airtight container. Use within a week, or store in the refrigerator.

Butternuts are sweeter than black walnuts but less common.

To crack the shells, you can buy a special black walnut cracker, but a hammer will do the trick. Place the nut pointed end up on a solid surface, and strike until it splits into sections. Covering the nut with a cloth will prevent flying shards. Nutmeats can be removed with a nut pick.

Use black walnuts in any recipe that calls for nuts. Refrigerate for short periods, or freeze for extended storage.

Found throughout the area but less common is the closely related white walnut, *J. cinerea*. Also known as butternut, it has an elongated nut. The husk is covered in sticky hairs, and its nutmeats are white. Butternuts are prepared in a similar fashion to black walnuts. Butternuts are the sweeter of the two. Nutritional profiles are similar. Harvest butternuts from the ground. There are no poisonous look-alikes to either species.

Black walnut wood is highly coveted, especially for making musical instruments and fine furniture.

The tree is infamous among gardeners, since it produces a toxic root chemical called juglone that prevents many other plants from growing beneath or near the tree. The zone of toxicity can extend 60 feet or more from the trunk. Black walnut definitely likes its own space.

Second year burdock, flowering

# BURDOCK
*Arctium minus* and *A. lappa*

**Family:** Asteraceae
**Also called:** Gobo, beggar's buttons
**Uses:** Flower stalk, root
**Cautions:** Look-alikes. Avoid if allergic to ragweed or other plants in the family, if pregnant/nursing, diabetic, or taking diuretics or blood thinners. Children should avoid.
**Season:** Summer, fall
**Range:** Throughout New Jersey and Pennsylvania; edges of woods, roadsides, waste places
**Description:** Biennial plant. Large leaves with wavy edges; may have tiny teeth, but not spiny. Leaves are dark green above and noticeably lighter and woolly beneath. Stem leaves are smaller than the ground-level rosette leaves. Stems round or slightly ridged, without blotches. Pink to purple flowers sit on top of a round bur composed of hooked spines. Mature burs stick to clothing and animal fur.

You may know burdock as a vile weed with tenacious burs that stick to your pants and your dog. But this annoying plant does have its good side and has been used by various cultures for centuries.

Two main species of burdock are found in the area; both are native to Europe. They are very similar except for their size. The smaller and more common burdock is *A. minus*. Great burdock (*A. lappa*) is similar in appearance, except it is a more robust plant reaching 9 feet tall with massive leaves and larger flowers. They have similar edible qualities.

The long taproot of burdock is the most commonly eaten part. It is famously known as *gobo* in Japanese cuisine. *A. lappa* is cultivated as a crop, and the root can grow to 3 feet long. *Gobo* is used in stir-fries and other dishes and is often pickled.

In its first year, burdock forms a rosette of large heart-shaped leaves at ground level. In its second year the plant puts up a tall flower stalk, which then forms prickly burs. The burs were actually the inspiration for the invention of Velcro in 1948.

To harvest burdock roots, dig the first-year plants in late summer or fall. In the second year they will be fibrous and woody. When digging, take care not to include roots of other plants growing near it. Using a spade or a digging fork, dig a hole next to the stalk of the plant. You may have to dig down a foot or more. Rinse the unearthed roots then peel, cut to desired size, and cook as a root vegetable. They can also be roasted and ground and used as a caffeine-free coffee substitute. People use terms like "earthy" when describing burdock root. To me it tastes like parsnip. Roots can be stored in the refrigerator for a week.

The flower stalk is also edible, but only at the immature stage before the flowers develop. The stalk will be solid inside, not hollow. Too tall,

The burs that inspired the invention of Velcro

Burdock has a deep taproot.

more than 2 feet or so, the stalk will be fibrous and inedible. To harvest, cut the stalk near the base. Peel off the outer bitter layer. The stalks have a taste reminiscent of artichoke and can be eaten raw or cooked. The young leaves can also be eaten but are bitter and need to be boiled in changes of water.

Native Americans used burdock to treat rheumatism. Burdock root has a history of use for many conditions, including reduction of blood sugar and treatment of infections. It is said to be a diuretic. Internet claims abound promoting burdock root to detoxify the liver. More research is necessary to verify efficacy or recommend burdock for use as medicine; few studies have been done on human subjects. To be safe, it is suggested that certain people not consume burdock (see "Cautions" above).

Burdock root is rich in inulin (not insulin), which acts as a prebiotic and promotes the growth of beneficial bacteria in the intestines. The root is also a source of carbohydrate calories, vitamin B6, potassium, copper, magnesium, and manganese. It is likely a healthful diet addition for most people.

There are look-alike plants to be aware of. In the rosette stage, common burdock resembles rhubarb (*Rheum* spp.), but the leaves of rhubarb are smooth and lack the wooly undersides. Cocklebur (*Xanthium* spp.) is another. Cocklebur has dark spots on the stems, and its leaves are sharply toothed, whereas burdock leaves have a wavy edge.

Leaves, seeds, and malodorous fruit of ginkgo

## GINKGO
*Ginkgo biloba*

**Family:** Ginkgoaceae
**Also called:** Gingko, maidenhair tree
**Uses:** Seeds, cooked; leaves used medicinally
**Cautions:** Fruit can cause contact dermatitis. Seeds in excess not advised.
**Season:** Autumn
**Range:** Widely planted in United States
**Description:** Deciduous tree, fan-shaped leaves about 3" across, notch divides leaf into 2 lobes, hence the species name *biloba*. Showy yellow fall foliage. Fruit about 1" across, tan-orange, round to oval, malodorous with 1 seed.

Ginkgo is a beautiful ornamental tree. Its leaves and seeds have known nutritional and healing properties. The oldest living species of tree in the world, it is considered a living fossil.

The leaves of ginkgo are not generally eaten, as they are very astringent. They are, however, used in the preparation of ginkgo biloba extract, a commercial supplement.

Ginkgo seeds may be harvested from the ground.

The flesh is inedible but contains a nutritious seed. To obtain these seeds (nuts), you must contend with the notoriously smelly flesh of the fruit. The odor has been variously described as rotten cheese, feces, or vomit. The flesh is known to cause contact dermatitis in some people.

Ginkgo has separate male and female trees. The females produce the fruit. For this reason, garden centers today only sell male trees. Because of complaints of the smell and messiness of dropped fruit, some towns, such as Easton, Pennsylvania, have removed many of their female ginkgo street trees.

When foraging ginkgo, it will likely be from trees found in parks, gardens, or street plantings. Ginkgo may be extinct in the wild. A few "wild" populations have been found in their native China, but they may actually have been planted by people long ago. The tree has been saved from extinction by human cultivation. Ginkgo has a very long life span and can live for more than 1,000 years. A champion *Ginkgo biloba* in Monmouth County, New Jersey, has a 216-foot circumference and stands 108 feet tall, the second largest in the United States.

A ginkgo seed in its tan shell looks very much like a pistachio. The shell is thin and easy to crack, and the nutmeat inside is a lovely green. The flavor of ginkgo nuts is pleasant, and I love the soft chewy texture. It is tempting to eat them by the handful, but eating large quantities is not advised. They contain a

**Cooked Ginkgo Nuts**

Put the nuts in a saucepan and cover with water. Boil for 15–20 minutes, or until the shells start to crack. Drain, then rinse under cold water. Crack the shells using a nut-cracker, or gently crush each one with the broad side of a knife. Discard the papery membrane that surrounds the nutmeat.

Some people crack or remove the shells before boiling. Either way works. Enjoy the cooked nuts plain, or add them to other dishes. Remember, moderation! They will keep in the refrigerator for a few days. Otherwise, store in the freezer.

chemical known as B6 antivitamin. Too much can deplete your body's supply of vitamin B6 and has been known to induce seizures when consumed in excess. Children and the elderly may be more susceptible.

Ginkgo seeds are considered a delicacy throughout Asia and are a common ingredient in Chinese vegetable dishes, congee, and desserts. The Hong Kong Department of Health Centre for Food Safety recognizes the potential hazards of this beloved food and advises limiting cooked seeds to a few per day and not eating them raw. Other sources issue similar cautions and variously suggest six, seven, ten seeds—there is no clearly defined limit. Cooking the seeds reduces but does not entirely eliminate the toxin.

Despite all the caveats, people around the world enjoy ginkgo nuts, and in moderate amounts they appear to benefit health. I guess it's similar to drinking red wine: If you chose to indulge, just don't overdo it.

The nuts are a source of niacin, vitamins A and C, potassium, and protein. They are low in sodium, carbohydrates, and fat.

Wearing rubber gloves while harvesting is wise. Ripe ginkgo fruits will fall from the tree. You may find plenty of mushed fruit on the ground with intact seeds, which are fine to take. Collect them in a bucket, then add water to separate the seeds from the pulp. With a gloved hand, swish them around and work the seeds free, then give them a final rinse. When clean they are OK to handle without gloves.

Ginkgo nuts are widely used in traditional Chinese medicine, often to treat breathing-related problems.

Ginkgo biloba extract is made from the leaves. It is a top-selling supplement in the United States and Europe, marketed mostly to enhance memory and improve blood circulation. Research does support ginkgo biloba extract as effective for mild cognitive impairment and dementia.

Ginkgo leaves are used to make a popular supplement.

Ginkgo trees were first brought to America by botanist William Hamilton. He imported three from London and planted two on his estate in Philadelphia. He gave the third tree to his naturalist friend William Bartram. This tree still survives at Bartram's Garden in Philadelphia and is believed to be the oldest ginkgo in North America.

Clusters of unripe grapes. Note the woody tendrils.

## GRAPE / WILD GRAPE
*Vitis* spp.

**Family:** Vitaceae

**Also called:** Fox grape, slipskin grape, summer grape, riverbank grape, frost grape

**Uses:** Leaves and fruit, raw or cooked

**Cautions:** Look-alikes

**Season:** Spring for leaves; summer for fruit

**Range:** Throughout New Jersey and Pennsylvania

**Description:** Thornless perennial vine with shredding bark when mature. Vines can get quite large. Leaves are simple, alternate, and coarsely toothed. Veins are palmate, extending from the petiole. Leaf shape varies but generally heart shaped or 3-lobed; there may be woolly hairs on the undersides. Forked tendrils are present. Small greenish flowers are inconspicuous. Fruit grows in hanging bunches, each ⅛"–1" across, dark purple to nearly black.

There are many species of wild grape in the United States, and a number of them grow in our area. Wild grape vines are everywhere. Walk the edges of any wooded area and you're likely to find grape. You may have pulled the weedy interlopers in your yard as they tried to gobble up your shrubs. Wild grape vines

Tendrils and serrated leaf edges help to identify wild grape.

can grow quite aggressively, climbing over and through surrounding vegetation, and up into tree canopies.

Most wild grape species are dioecious, with separate male and female plants. Both are required within close proximity for the females to produce fruit.

Wild grapes are usually smaller and more tart than commercial grapes, but some are large and luscious. The plant climbs by using forked tendrils—thin, threadlike stems that coil around other objects. Tendrils start out tender and green and become woody and brittle with age.

A few plants are sometimes mistaken for grape. Moonseed (*Menispermum canadense*) is toxic, and its fruit looks similar to grape. But moonseed does not

## RECIPE

**Wild Grape Juice**

Abundantly found riverside grapes work well in this recipe.

Harvest at least 1 gallon of grapes. Rinse. Remove stems and unripe or damaged grapes. Put grapes in a large pot and add water to barely cover. Simmer gently for 10 minutes, mashing to release juices. Let cool for a few minutes. Strain juice by putting a sieve over a jar. Refrigerate the juice for two days. Tartaric acid crystals will settle to the bottom. They are safe to eat but gritty. Slowly pour the juice off into a fresh pitcher or jar, discarding the crystals. Add sugar and/or water to the juice as desired.

have tendrils, and its leaves do not have serrated edges. Moonseed berries have a single crescent-shaped seed, while grapes have rounded seeds.

Virginia creeper (*Parthenocissus quinquefolia*) has small dark berries, but its leaves are compound with five leaflets to a stem. Grape has one solid leaf. Boston ivy (*Parthenocissus tricuspidata*) also has grapelike fruits, but its tendrils have small disks used to adhere to surfaces.

The most common wild grapes in New Jersey and Pennsylvania are riverbank, summer, and fox grapes. The one you're more likely to find is the riverbank grape (*V. riparia*). The fruit is pea size with a bloom (waxy coating). The leaves have two small side lobes and are coarsely toothed. Leaf undersides are hairy along the veins. Riverbank grapes are acidic, but will sweeten after a frost.

Fox grapes (*V. labrusca*) are relatively large, about ¾ inch across. The flavor is sweet and described as musky or foxy. The leaf underside is covered with rusty colored hairs. Fox grape is a parent to the famous Concord grape. This variety of *V. labrusca* has an extraordinary antioxidant value due to polyphenols like resveratrol, known as a longevity nutrient.

Summer grape (*V. aestivalis*) is a small grape, about ¼–½ inch. The leaf undersides have cobwebby hairs.

Pennsylvania is home to the sand grape (*V. rupestris*). This rare species was thought to be extirpated in the state but is now listed as endangered due to its recent rediscovery. It occurs on protected lands in western Pennsylvania. Unlike most grapes, sand grape is small, shrubby, and non-vining. It is notable as one of two species credited for saving the European wine industry in the late 1800s.

Toxic moonseed does not have tendrils, and the leaf edges are smooth not serrated.

Riverbank grapes are abundant in New Jersey and Pennsylvania.

Commercial grapes were nearly wiped out by an aphid called phylloxera, and the rootstock of sand grape was used to grow more resistant vines.

Dark-skinned grapes are rich in antioxidants. Research has shown that wild grape species have very high levels of polyphenols, about two to ten times that of cultivated grapes (*V. vinifera*). These substances can lower inflammation and reduce risk of cancer, diabetes, and heart disease.

Grape leaves are also nutritious. Stuffed grape leaves are an iconic Mediterranean dish.

Ground cherries in their lantern-like husks, still green

# GROUND CHERRY
*Physalis* spp.

**Family:** Solanaceae

**Also called:** Groundcherry, husk tomato, strawberry tomato, cape gooseberry, bladder cherry

**Uses:** Ripe fruit, raw or cooked

**Cautions:** Leaves, husks, and unripe fruit should not be eaten.

**Season:** Late summer, autumn

**Range:** Throughout New Jersey and Pennsylvania; disturbed or gravelly areas, roadsides, fields, woodland edges; sun to part shade

**Description:** Branching plant, about 1'–2' high. Leaves are alternate; may be entire, irregularly toothed, or slightly lobed. Yellow cup- or bell-shaped flower with a dark center. Fruit is a round tomato-like berry enclosed in an inflated calyx that resembles a paper lantern. The berry is about ½" across, and ranges from gold or orange to purplish when ripe, with many small seeds inside.

Ground cherries are not actually cherries. They're members of the nightshade family, which includes eggplant, peppers, and tomato. They resemble tiny tomatoes. When ripe, ground cherries are sweet, with a flavor often described as tomato-like with notes of pineapple or strawberry.

The most distinguishing feature of the plant is the papery covering that encloses the fruit. This lantern-like husk makes ground cherry easy to identify.

Ripe ground cherry in its husk

Ripe ground cherry

All members of the *Physalis* genus produce edible fruit. They were a common food of Native Americans.

The exact number of species is debated. Common in this area are the smooth ground cherry (*P. subglabrata*), and clammy ground cherry (*P. heterophylla*), which has hairy leaves and stems. Cape gooseberry (*P. peruviana*), native to South America, is a popular cultivated ground cherry. The tomatillo (*P. philadelphica*), frequently used in Mexican cuisine, is a *Physalis* crop species that bears relatively large fruits. The Chinese lantern plant (*P. alkekengi*), with its showy bright orange-red husks, is grown as an ornamental. Its fruit is also edible.

Ground cherries are nutritious. Analysis of *P. peruviana* fruit reveals high levels of beneficial compounds including dietary fiber, vitamin K1, vitamin E, beta-carotene, vitamin C, iron and B-complex vitamins, and significant amounts of magnesium and zinc. The iron content is greater than that of beans, and vitamin C was measured at 46 mg/100 g, which is higher than most fruits and comparable to orange and strawberry.

Compounds called withanolides have been discovered in ground cherry plants, some of them demonstrating potent anticancer activity and anti-microbial and anti-inflammatory properties.

When ripe, the ground cherry husk turns tan and dry. The fruit, in its husk, will often fall from the plant before it is ripe and will continue to ripen on the ground (or on your counter). The mature fruit is sweet with no bitterness. Unripe fruit can cause upset stomach, vomiting, or diarrhea. If the berry tastes bitter or objectionable, don't eat it.

Ground cherries work in both sweet and savory dishes. Remove the husk and eat as is, or incorporate into recipes for salsa, jam, or pie. Toss the berries into a salad, or use as a garnish. The berries can also be dried to make "raisins." Dipped in chocolate, ground cherries are a real treat. If you like chocolate-covered cherries, try this recipe.

Ground cherry in March, remnant from previous year

For storage, it's best to leave fresh berries in their husks. They will last for several weeks refrigerated or in a cool, well-ventilated place.

The yellow berries of horse nettle (*Solanum carolinense*) look similar to ground cherries, but they are not contained in a husk. They are poisonous and should be avoided. Ground cherry fruit will always have a husk.

Ground cherries are pollinated by a variety of bees. The fruit is enjoyed by wildlife including turkeys, skunks, opossum, foxes, and eastern box turtles.

## RECIPE

### Chocolate-Kissed Ground Cherries

Ground cherries, husks peeled back but still attached (They need to be dry, or the chocolate will become grainy.)
8-ounce bar chocolate (dark or milk), chopped small

Line a tray with a sheet of wax paper or parchment. Put the chocolate in a small microwavable bowl. Microwave on medium for about 2 minutes. Stir until smooth. Do not overheat. Using the husk as a handle, dip each dry berry into the melted chocolate. Place on the lined tray and let set at room temperature for 20–30 minutes.

Hackberry leaves are finely separated and have a lopsided base.

## HACKBERRY
*Celtis* spp.

**Family:** Cannabaceae (formerly Ulmacaeae)

**Also called:** Common hackberry, northern hackberry, sugarberry, nettle tree

**Uses:** Fruit, raw or cooked

**Cautions:** No poisonous look-alikes

**Season:** Fall

**Range:** Throughout; more common in northern New Jersey and southern Pennsylvania; mixed deciduous woodlands, riverbanks, parks, fencerows. Occurs as scattered individual trees.

**Description:** Deciduous tree, to 80'. The fruits are pea-size berries and are dark red, purple, or purple-brown when ripe in fall. They may persist on the tree into spring. A thin layer of flesh surrounds a large seed. Leaves are 2½"–6" long with a pointed tip and finely toothed edges. The leaf is asymmetrical with a lopsided base. Leaves very often covered with nipple galls caused by small insects; these are so prevalent that they assist in identification of the tree. Small light green flowers in spring. Mature bark is gray-brown with distinctive warty ridges.

Hackberries have a pleasant, sweet flavor similar to dates. A thin layer of sugary flesh surrounds a large seed. The berries may trigger disappointment in someone expecting a fleshy fruit, but savoring a ripe hackberry is a good exercise in mindful eating.

The seed of a hackberry is edible but very hard. Some people actually do chew them. I prefer to eat the flesh off the pit and spit out the seed. Processing the whole berries into a "milk" is another way to enjoy the flavor and nutritional goodness of this wild food.

Hackberries are quite nutritious and are one of the oldest known plant foods eaten and stored by humans. The remains of hackberry seed caches were found

Hackberries in July. When ripe, the nutritious berries will be dark red, purple, or purple-brown.

The typical warty bark of a hackberry tree

in caves occupied by our early human ancestors over a half million years ago. The seeds are also found in abundance in archaeological sites in North America. Hackberry seeds were the most common type of plant remains found at Meadowcroft Rockshelter, a prehistoric campsite in what is now western Pennsylvania. Human use of the shelter dates back at least 16,000 years.

Native Americans made great use of hackberries. In addition to eating them fresh, they also pounded and crushed them fine with added fat and mixed this with other foods. Hackberries were dried and stored for winter use. Native peoples used the tree medicinally as well. Hackberry bark was boiled down into an extract used to treat sore throat and menstrual problems. Whole hackberry fruits are rich in calcium, potassium, manganese, selenium, magnesium, and zinc. They contain 19 percent protein.

Harvesting hackberries from high branches may be difficult. Use a stick to shake the branches and dislodge ripe fruits. The berries can sometimes remain on the tree until spring. Due to their low moisture and high sugar content, they are resistant to spoilage.

At least six species of hackberry grow in North America. All have edible fruit. In this area, the most common by far is the common or northern hackberry (*C. occidentalis*). A state champion tree in Montgomery County, Pennsylvania, has measured 106 feet. A common hackberry in Warren County, New Jersey, is the state champion, standing at 211 feet, and it may be the tallest in the country. Dwarf hackberry (*C. tenuifolia*) is a smaller tree found mainly in southeastern Pennsylvania. It also has warty bark, and only grows to about 25 feet.

The hackberry tree is the host plant for the hackberry emperor butterfly (*Asterocampa celtis*). The pretty brown butterfly lays its eggs on the leaves, which are the only food source for its larvae.

Spring leaves, flower buds, and flowers are edible.

## HAWTHORN
*Crataegus* spp.

**Family:** Rosaceae
**Also called:** Haw, quickthorn, thornapple, May-tree, whitethorn
**Uses:** Leaves, flower buds, young flowers, fruits
**Cautions:** Thorns, seeds
**Season:** Leaves, flower buds, young flowers in spring; fruits in late summer, early fall
**Range:** Throughout New Jersey and Pennsylvania; sunny fields, along roads, fences, edges of woods
**Description:** Deciduous small tree, 15'–30' tall. Leaves alternate, sharply serrated, often lobed. Branches have huge thorns, 2"–4" long, straight, or slightly curved. Small white or pale pink flowers in spring, 5 petals. Fruit is a small pome about ¼" across, red when ripe. Mealy pulp. Number of seeds varies.

Hawthorn has a long history of edible and medicinal use around the world. There are more than 200 *Crataegus* species worldwide. The exact number is uncertain, as they crossbreed extensively and are a challenge to differentiate and classify.

The fruits and leaves were eaten by Native Americans for centuries. Hawthorn was regarded as medicine for various ailments and primarily viewed as a heart tonic.

In some European countries, the hawthorn tree is known as "bread and cheese," alluding to its edible leaves and fruits. The fruits and flowers have been shown to contain vitamin C in varying amounts depending on species, growing location, and other environmental factors.

A member of the rose family, hawthorn fruits resemble rose hips or tiny apples. Sometimes called haws, they can be eaten off the tree. Flavor varies greatly, but they can be delicious. The fresh new leaves, flower buds, and young flowers are nice in salads. The fruits are made into sauces, jam, and jelly.

While hawthorn fruit is safe and nutritious, the seeds should not be eaten. They contain a toxic substance called amygdalin, found naturally in the pits of many fruits, including apples. Treat hawthorn seeds like apple seeds. Hawthorn fruits can be cooked whole to make jelly and other recipes—simply strain out the seeds. If eating raw fruits, spit out the seeds, and don't chew them.

Hawthorn is well known in the traditional medicine of many cultures and has been used for a variety of maladies, mostly heart-related. A growing body of scientific evidence supports such use. Analysis of fruits, flowers, and leaves shows them to be rich in many compounds, including flavonoids and procyanidins, powerful antioxidants known to be protective against heart disease and other conditions. A meta-analysis of double-blind studies confirmed significant improvement in people with chronic heart failure symptoms such as shortness of breath and fatigue when hawthorn extract was used along with conventional

Hawthorn fruit is nutritious. Discard the seeds.

Hawthorn fruits, flowers, and leaves contain powerful antioxidants.

treatment. Researchers see the plant as having significant potential in the treatment of heart disease, with an excellent safety profile.

Hawthorn is frequently planted for its ornamental beauty. There are no poisonous look-alikes. Look for the key identifying features of very long sharp thorns, serrated leaf margins, and red apple-like fruits. Many cultivars have been developed, and some bear yellow fruit.

## RECIPE

**Hawthorn Syrup**

About 2 cups fresh hawthorn fruit
Juice of 1 lemon
¼ cup or more sweetener of choice (sugar, honey, or maple syrup)

Place fruit into a medium saucepan and add sufficient water to cover by at least 1 inch. Bring to a boil, then reduce to a simmer. Gently cook for about 1 hour with the lid ajar, until the fruit is very soft, adding water if necessary to prevent sticking. Strain out the mash and seeds, reserving the liquid, then return the liquid to the pot. Cook further if you wish to reduce the volume. Remove from heat. Add lemon juice and sweeten as desired. Transfer into a clean jar and refrigerate. Will keep for about two weeks. This is a food. No claims are made for its therapeutic properties, although it can't hurt!

Hawthorn thorns are very sharp, and may be up to 4 inches long.

The dense thorny branches provide sanctuary for wildlife. Songbirds such as cedar waxwings eat the fruit, and caterpillars of several types of butterflies feed on the leaves.

Hawthorn has been planted as a living fence to confine livestock. The word "haw" comes from an Old English term meaning "hedge," so, "hedge thorn."

Note the rounded leaf lobes of white oak.

## OAK / ACORN
*Quercus* spp.

**Family:** Fagaceae
**Also called:** Red, white, black, bur, post, chestnut oak
**Uses:** Acorns edible after leaching
**Cautions:** Tree nut allergies. Raw or unprocessed acorns.
**Season:** Fall
**Range:** Throughout New Jersey and Pennsylvania
**Description:** Deciduous trees 50'–80' tall. A variety of leaf shapes, depending on species. Leaves are simple, alternate, usually lobed or toothed; shingle oak and willow oak are smooth edged. The fruit is an acorn, a thin-shelled nut with a cap. Acorns start out green and turn brown as they ripen. Sizes ½"–2".

Many people are surprised when they find out that acorns are edible. For thousands of years, acorns have been an important food source wherever oak trees are found. All species of oak produce edible acorns. The nuts are a good source of protein, fiber, and vitamin E, and are an excellent source of provitamin A. They have significant levels of iron, zinc, copper, manganese, magnesium, calcium, and potassium.

Acorns are high in tannins, astringent compounds also found in tea, coffee, and wine. These substances possess health benefits but are toxic if consumed in large amounts. To make acorns palatable and safe, the bitter tannins need to be

Tiny holes are a sign of acorn weevils.

leached out. The nuts are soaked in changes of water or boiled. Once processed, acorns are perfectly safe to eat.

Oaks are divided into two basic groups: white oaks, which have rounded leaf lobes, and red oaks, with bristle-tipped lobes. Acorns in the red oak group have more tannins. Either way, all acorns need to be leached before eating.

To forage acorns, collect them from the ground. Don't take green, unripe acorns or any with pinpoint holes, which are a sign of acorn weevils. Most of

Ripe acorns

the acorns you find will be without caps. That's fine. A tightly adhering cap means the acorn is not ripe. Acorns can also be shaken from the branches, dislodging ones that are ready to fall.

To transform acorns into good food, shell them, grind them, and then leach. Drying acorns makes it easier to remove the shells. Spread them on a baking sheet and heat in a 200°F oven for 30 minutes.

To shell acorns, crack them with a nutcracker or a hammer. Remove the nutmeats and grind in a food processor until a consistency of coarse corn meal or grits is achieved. The smaller the pieces, the larger the surface area, and the quicker your acorns will leach.

A bur oak acorn has a large shaggy cap.

My preferred method is cold-water leaching. While boiling may be quicker, it causes the nutritious oils to be lost, and the heat causes a change in flavor that I do not prefer.

Fill a large jar no more than one-half full with acorn meal. Top off with cold water. Put the jar in the fridge. Some people do this process at room temperature, but I prefer to keep the jar refrigerated for food safety reasons. Change the water at least once a day. After a few days, taste a piece or two. If still bitter, continue leaching. It takes time, maybe more than a week. When most of the tannins are leached out and the taste is agreeable, this step is complete. Drain your acorn meal through a fine strainer.

## RECIPE

**Acorn Grits (or "Oak Meal")**

1½ cups water
Pinch of salt
½ cup freshly made acorn meal

Bring the water to a boil. Stir in the salt and acorn meal. Cook gently until thickened, stirring occasionally. Add butter, salt, and pepper to taste. Topped with a poached egg, this makes a lovely meal.

Northern red oak with unripe acorn

Acorn meal can be used at this point, or dried and stored for future use. If you grind it further, you will have acorn flour, which can be incorporated into baked goods. Acorns are naturally gluten free.

About eighteen species of oak occur in the New Jersey–Pennsylvania area. Bur oak (*Q. macrocarpa*) has the largest acorn of all native oaks. The northern red oak (*Q. rubra*) is the state tree of New Jersey.

The bark of oak trees has been used in traditional medicine to treat diarrhea, skin conditions, and other ailments. Research has shown that oak tree bark contains a number of phenolic compounds that have antioxidant, antimicrobial, and anticancer properties.

Acorns are an important food source for bears, deer, blue jays, woodpeckers, squirrels, and many other critters.

Partridge berry with dimples

## PARTRIDGE BERRY
*Mitchella repens*

**Family:** Rubiaceae
**Also called:** Partridgeberry, squaw vine, twinberry, two-eyed berry
**Uses:** Berries eaten out of hand, nice as a garnish; leaves and berries used for tea
**Cautions:** Safety of medicinal uses
**Season:** Berries form in summer but often persist through winter; leaves year-round.
**Range:** Throughout New Jersey and Pennsylvania, often in the shade of conifer trees
**Description:** Trailing ground cover, forms mat-like colonies on the forest floor. Leathery evergreen leaves are arranged oppositely on the stem; leaves have a white or yellowish midvein; leaf edges are smooth. Fuzzy, white, trumpet-shaped fragrant flowers in spring followed by bright red berries, each containing 8 seeds.

Here's a weird fun fact. It takes two flowers to make each partridge berry! The little white flowers grow in pairs, fused at the base. If both flowers are fertilized, one berry will result. See the two dimples on a partridge berry? Those are the remnants of the flowers. So unique!

Partridge berry grows close to the forest floor. It spreads and forms mats of foliage that are often covered by fallen leaves. The species name, *repens*, is Latin for "creeping."

The edible berries are long-lasting. You can still find them in winter or spring if no one has eaten them. They don't have much flavor but are a fun trail nibble.

They work well as a neutral-tasting but showy garnish for desserts and other dishes and are sometimes made into jam.

The leaves are used for tea, but usually for medicinal reasons and not so much as a tasty beverage. The plant has a very long history of use by Native American women. It was used extensively to alleviate discomfort in the last months of pregnancy and to facilitate delivery in childbirth. There is, however, virtually no research on the safety of partridge berry for labor induction. The common name squaw vine is falling out of favor; some consider "squaw" to be a derogatory term used for American Indian women.

Partridge berry is still used by some practitioners of herbal medicine for a wide array of conditions: anxiety, diarrhea, kidney failure, water retention (as a diuretic), and to enhance fertility. Again, very little scientific research has been conducted on this plant, and there is insufficient evidence to support its use as medicine.

Partridge berries may be tasteless, but that doesn't mean they're useless. The berries are said to be high in vitamin C and antioxidants, although nutrient analysis is scarce. The pigments that give all edible berries their vibrant red and purple colors are actually powerful antioxidants. Being a bright red edible berry, partridge berry is bound to have similar disease-fighting capabilities.

Bright red berry pigments are antioxidants.

**Partridge Berry Fruit Salad**

Small handful of partridge berries
1 apple, chopped
1 kiwi, peeled and diced
½ cup seedless grapes, halved
Vanilla yogurt for topping

Combine all fruits in a mixing bowl. Top with a dollop of yogurt.

Partridge berry does have a look-alike plant. Wintergreen (*Gaultheria procumbens*) has the same low-growing mat-forming habit. Both plants have red berries that persist through the winter, and small evergreen leaves that grow in the same type of habitat. You'll often see the two plants side by side along woodland trails. Wintergreen leaves are a bit larger, and are alternate on the stem, not opposite like partridge berry. Luckily, wintergreen is also edible, so no problem if you get the two confused.

Partridge berries are eaten by ruffed grouse, northern bobwhite, wild turkey, foxes, white-footed mice, and skunks. The plant is native to eastern North America. The genus name honors John Mitchell, an early American botanist from Virginia.

Partridge berry is sometimes used as an ornamental ground cover. Although it is still a fairly common plant in many eastern states, caution is advised in removing it from its natural environment. It has become a threatened species in Iowa.

A handful of pawpaws

## PAWPAW
*Asimina triloba*

**Family:** Annonaceae
**Also called:** Hoosier banana, poor man's banana, Indian banana, false banana, custard apple
**Uses:** Ripe fruit, raw or cooked
**Cautions:** Do not eat skin, seeds, or unripe fruit; possible adverse reactions.
**Season:** September through early October
**Range:** Southern Pennsylvania, scattered occurrences in New Jersey; moist bottomlands, wooded slopes, along rivers and streams. Forms colonies, or "patches."
**Description:** Small understory tree, to 30'. Leaves are green, alternate, drooping, oblong with smooth edges and a pointed tip. They are up to 1' long, wider above the center. Fall leaves are golden. Maroon colored flowers in spring, 1"–1½". Fruit 3"–6" long, green, turning yellow with dark spots when ripe. Flesh is yellow, with 2 rows of brown/black seeds that look like large beans.

Pawpaw is the largest edible fruit native to North America. Its range covers most of the eastern United States and parts of Canada. The luscious fruit has a long history of use as food. Native Americans not only foraged and ate the pawpaw but also cultivated the trees and introduced the fruits to European settlers. It is said that George Washington enjoyed pawpaws for dessert, Thomas Jefferson grew pawpaw trees at Monticello, and the Lewis and Clark Expedition foraged and ate pawpaws when their rations ran low. Botanist John Bartram grew pawpaw trees in his garden near Philadelphia.

Pawpaw has a smooth texture, and a flavor often described as tropical and likened to pineapple, banana, or mango. Pawpaws are eaten raw and sometimes incorporated into desserts. They work well as a substitute for ripe bananas in recipes. A pawpaw is ripe and ready when it is slightly soft.

Pawpaws are a very good source of potassium, vitamin C, magnesium, and iron. They also contain B vitamins, calcium, and beta-carotene.

They can be collected from the ground, or you can shake the tree very gently to dislodge ripe fruits. This is a good two-person job: One person nudges the tree, and the other tries to catch the falling fruits or at least break their fall. A ripe pawpaw can squish easily on impact. Put them in a single layer in a shallow container or box. If picked from the tree when hard and unripe, pawpaws will not continue to ripen.

Pawpaw seeds and skin are not edible.

Some people develop stomach upset after eating pawpaw. So eat only a little at first. The leaves can cause skin irritation in sensitive individuals.

Pawpaws contain healthful compounds that have anticancer, antiviral, and antimicrobial properties. The polyphenols and antioxidant activity compare favorably to other fruits. Pawpaw also contains annonacin, a neurotoxin. It is not yet clear if this constitutes a risk. There are varied opinions in the scientific community, and more research has been called for. Moderation may be key. I will continue to enjoy these nutritious seasonal treats as I find them.

Pawpaw pulp can be used in baked goods.

Pawpaws in mid-October, the last of the season

The zebra swallowtail (*Protographium marcellus*), also known as the pawpaw butterfly, relies on the tree for survival. Its caterpillars feed only on pawpaw

Pawpaw leaves can cause skin irritation in some people.

leaves. Pawpaw flowers are an unusual maroon color. They have a faint smell of rotting meat, which serves to attract beetles and carrion flies, which also feed on dead animals. To me the flowers also look like meat.

Pawpaw flowers smell like rotting meat to attract carrion flies and beetles for pollination.

## RECIPE

**Pawpaw Breakfast Cookies**

1¼ cups quick oats
1 cup pawpaw pulp
½ teaspoon cinnamon
¼ cup peanut butter
¼ cup finely chopped walnuts (optional)

Preheat oven to 350°F. Mix all ingredients together. (Add a bit more flour if necessary, to make a soft dough consistency.) Take a cookie-size amount of dough and roll into a ball. Place on parchment-lined or greased cookie sheet. Flatten each ball slightly. Bake for 12–15 minutes. To fancy them up a bit, press a few chocolate chips into each or roll in coconut flakes before baking.

Ripe persimmons are nature's candy.

## PERSIMMON
*Diospyros virginiana*

**Family:** Ebenaceae
**Also called:** American persimmon, common persimmon, wild persimmon, possumwood
**Uses:** Ripe fruit, raw or cooked; leaves for tea
**Cautions:** Eat only very ripe fruit.
**Season:** Fall
**Range:** Throughout New Jersey, southern and central Pennsylvania; prefers moist soil but also found in dry areas, open woods, old fields, fencerows, near streams
**Description:** Deciduous tree, 35'–60' or taller. Branches are alternate. Leaves are dark green, oval, simple, 2"–5½", with smooth margins. They may turn yellow, orange, or red in autumn. Flowers are creamy white to greenish, urn-shaped, blooming in late April–May. Male and female flowers are on separate trees; females produce fleshy, round, orange or reddish fruits, 1"–1½" across, which ripen in autumn. Each contains 0–8 seeds and is crowned with a 4-lobed calyx. Bark at maturity is dark gray, rugged, divided into squarish blocks.

Persimmons are nature's candy. When fully ripe, American persimmons are sweet, with a sugar content higher than that of ripe bananas. The wild fruit is

**Persimmon Fruit Leather**

Persimmon fruit pulp

**Food dehydrator:** Line the tray of a food dehydrator with parchment paper (unless your dehydrator comes with a special fruit roll tray). Spread persimmon pulp very thinly onto the parchment. Dry at 145°F, or follow your machine's instructions. It will take at least 6 hours. Finished fruit leather should be dry and no longer tacky.

    **Oven:** Line a baking sheet with parchment, spread out the pulp, and dry at the lowest setting (150°F or 170°F), leaving the door ajar.

    Finished fruit leather can be rolled up and cut into pieces. Store in plastic wrap or airtight containers in a cool dry place.

quite small compared to the Asian persimmon found in supermarkets. Although smaller than a golf ball, the diminutive native fruits are sugar bombs.

    Persimmons were widely eaten by native peoples, who enjoyed them fresh, cooked into sweet dishes, and dried for storage. European settlers were fond of the fruits as well, and persimmon pudding became a popular dish.

Note the blocky "alligator bark."

An underripe persimmon is high in tannins and extremely astringent. It will make your mouth feel very bad. To safely consume, the fruit should be very ripe. It will look almost spoiled. A soft and wrinkly persimmon is deliciously sweet.

Wild persimmon is easy to spot by its unusual blocky bark. Don't pick persimmons off the tree. Ripe fruits will be on the ground. You can spread a clean tarp under the tree to collect fallen fruits or gently agitate the branches to facilitate the process.

Fallen fruits. These are perfectly ripe.

Wash the fruit, remove the calyx, and enjoy persimmons out of hand, or make pulp to use for muffins, breads, smoothies, jam, or fruit leather. Substitute persimmon pulp where a fruit pulp or pumpkin puree might be called for. Persimmon pulp freezes well. To separate the pulp from the seeds, use a food mill, a large-holed strainer, or a cone sieve with pestle. Dried persimmon was an important winter staple for Native Americans and settlers.

It's a common misconception that persimmons need a frost to ripen. I have found and eaten perfectly luscious fruits before any frost occurred.

Wild persimmons contain more vitamin C, potassium, iron, and calcium than cultivated Asian persimmons. The wild variety has more vitamin C than citrus fruit, averaging 86 mg per 100 g. Ripe fruits average 26 percent carbohydrates, 1.7 percent fat, and 0.6 percent protein.

The orange-red color of a ripe persimmon is due to carotenoid pigments, which act as antioxidants. These compounds help to maintain overall health, visual function, and a healthy immune system.

Persimmon bark has a long history of traditional uses. It was chewed by native peoples to relieve heartburn, and bark infusions were used for sore throat, fever, mouth sores, diarrhea, and as a skin wash.

The leaves have been used to make a tasty caffeine-free tea. Persimmon leaves are vitamin C rich, and research shows that an infusion, or tea, of the leaves is high in antioxidant activity. Persimmon seeds have been roasted and used as a coffee substitute.

The tree produces a dark, fine-grained wood used for making golf club heads and billiard cues.

The flowers are pollinated by wind and insects. Persimmon is a host tree for luna moth caterpillars.

Rose petals are beautiful and edible.

## ROSE
*Rosa* spp.

**Family:** Rosaceae
**Also called:** Wild rose
**Uses:** Leaves, petals, fruits
**Cautions:** Thorns. Plants may have been sprayed. Rose allergies. Seed hairs may be irritating.
**Season:** Spring through fall
**Range:** Various species and varieties throughout New Jersey and Pennsylvania; sunny edges of woodlands, fields, roadsides
**Description:** Leaves alternate, pinnate with odd number of leaflets. Leaflets oval with serrated edges. Thick canes (stems) have thorns or prickles. Flowers pink or white with 5 petals. Fruit round or oval, orange to red in color.

All roses, wild and cultivated, are edible. From the petals to young leaves and rose fruits, the plant offers a wide range of nutrients for humans.

The rose fruit is known as a rose hip. The hip forms after the flower fades. While rose petals and leaves contain vitamin C and nutrients, the hips get most of the attention, and for good reason. Rose hips show higher antioxidant activity than other well-known antioxidant fruits such as chokeberry, black currant, and blueberry. Antioxidants can reduce risk of cancer, maintain heart health, and stave off the effects of aging. Analysis also confirms that the hips contain high levels of vitamins C, E, and carotenoids.

Rose hips are the fruit of the rose.

Rose hips should be harvested when ripe and dark orange to red, depending on the rose species. Squeeze the hip; it should give between your fingers. Taste one. If ripe, it should have some flavor.

Rose hips can be eaten raw, like a tiny apple (they are in the same family). The seeds inside, however, contain hairs that may be irritating to the gastrointestinal tract of some people. If the hip is large enough, cut it in half, then use your finger or a small spoon to remove the seeds. The fleshy pulp can be used for sauce or jam. Some rose hips are too small and fiddly to separate the seeds out,

## RECIPE

**Rose Hip Syrup**

2 cups rose hips
1 cup water
½ cup sugar

Using a knife or food processor, roughly chop the hips. Transfer to a saucepan and add the water; simmer for 20 minutes. When hips are tender, strain through a colander. To remove any tiny seed hairs, strain again through a jelly bag, muslin, double layer of cheesecloth, or a coffee filter. Return the rose hip liquid to the saucepan. Add the sugar. Heat until the sugar is dissolved and the sauce has thickened a bit. Refrigerate syrup until ready to use.

Multiflora rose hips in winter

in which case I recommend cooking the hips, then straining the seeds to make tea or syrup.

Fresh rose petals can be added to salad or used as an attractive garnish for desserts. Rose petals and flower buds make a nice caffeine-free tea. The flavor is floral. Rose leaves can also be used for tea, and although the taste is not flowery, it still makes a nourishing hot beverage. Petals, leaves, and hips can be used in fresh or dried form.

Roses have no poisonous look-alikes. However, those from a florist should not be consumed as they have likely been treated with preservatives or other chemicals.

Multiflora rose (*R. multiflora*) is a notorious rose that you should have no trouble finding. Acknowledged as an invasive plant, multiflora rose, also known as baby rose or Japanese rose, was introduced into Pennsylvania in the 1930s as rootstock for grafted ornamental roses. It was originally employed as a crash barrier along highways, as vegetation to prevent erosion, and as a "living fence" to confine cattle. Until the 1960s, biologists recommended it for habitat restoration to provide food and shelter for wildlife. We now know better. The aggressive nature of multiflora rose creates dense thickets and displaces native vegetation.

In 1982 multiflora rose was listed as a noxious weed in Pennsylvania, and it is illegal to sell it in the state.

As foragers often say of invasive plants, if you can't beat 'em, eat 'em. Multiflora rose has a lot going for it nutritionally, with a vitamin and antioxidant profile similar to its more well-behaved relatives. It blooms May–June with small, fragrant white flowers. The hips are about ¼ inch across, and bright red at maturity. They may persist on the plant through winter.

To identify multiflora rose, look for fringed stipules at the base of each leaf stalk. These feathery appendages, along with white flower clusters, distinguish it from native roses.

Winter spicebush twigs, ready to make some refreshing tea

## SPICEBUSH
*Lindera benzoin*

**Family:** Lauraceae
**Also called:** Northern spicebush, Appalachian allspice, wild allspice, Benjamin bush, fever bush
**Uses:** All aboveground parts, raw or cooked
**Cautions:** None
**Season:** Year-round
**Range:** Throughout Pennsylvania and New Jersey; understory plant, common along streams, woodland clearings, trailsides, field edges
**Description:** Deciduous shrub. Twigs are olive green to brownish. Winter twigs have round floral buds. Bark is smooth with small light-colored lenticels. Small yellow flowers appear in spring, followed by leaves. Leaves are green, slightly paler below, soft, smooth edged, elliptical, about 3"–5" in length, alternate on the stem. Fruit is shiny, bright red when ripe, oblong, usually under ½" long, and contains a single seed. A pleasant spicy-citrusy fragrance is released when any part of the plant is crushed.

One of the things I like most about spicebush, in addition to its heady fragrance, is the fact that it is available to forage all year long. Even when there are no fruits or leaves, the bare twigs make a warming winter beverage or a refreshing iced spicebush tea.

Once you know the intoxicating smell of spicebush, it's easy to confirm its identity, even in winter. If you think you've found it, just give it the scratch-and-sniff test. Scratching a twig or crushing a leaf will let you know you've got the right plant.

During foraging programs, I've had a number of woodland owners question me on the native status of spicebush, citing dense colonies and a weedy nature. The native shrub can be found in great abundance when it's happy in a location.

Spicebush berries ripen in late summer. They are intensely flavored and not the kind of fruit you would eat a handful of. Spicebush berries straddle the sweet/savory culinary categories and are used in baked goods, in ice cream, and as a meat seasoning. Americans have used them since colonial days as an allspice substitute.

The flesh of the berry is slightly sweet; the seed is rather peppery. Separating the two is tedious, so the whole berry is usually ground. Spicebush berries can be dried and stored. Use a food dehydrator, or dry them in an oven at the lowest setting with the door ajar. Spicebush berries are rich in oil, which can oxidize and become rancid, so keep them refrigerated or in the freezer.

Characteristic spicebush bark with lenticels

Unopened floral buds in April

Unripe berries and foliage in July

Ripe, glossy red spicebush berries

Retrieve small amounts as needed, and grind them in a coffee grinder as you would other spices.

Traditionally the plant has been used by Native Americans and European settlers for food and medicine. They drank spicebush tea as a tonic and took infusions of the leaves and twigs for colds, coughs, and fever. Spicebush is thought to be diaphoretic, meaning that it induces sweating. The bark was used to treat intestinal parasites, and it is said that rubbing crushed spicebush leaves on the skin deters mosquitoes.

Science suggests some medicinal qualities of spicebush. Research has shown that extract of spicebush bark strongly inhibits the fungal organism *Candida albicans* as well as *Trichophyton rubrum*, a fungus that causes athlete's foot.

Spicebush is an important host plant for the spicebush swallowtail butterfly, whose caterpillar feeds on the leaves. The berries have a high fat and calorie content, ideal for sustaining migrating birds.

Staghorn sumac bob with red berries. Note the serrated leaflets.

## STAGHORN SUMAC
*Rhus typhina*

**Family:** Anacardiaceae
**Also called:** Sumach, staghorn, velvet sumac, lemonade tree
**Uses:** Berries, as spice or beverage
**Cautions:** None
**Season:** Late summer, fall
**Range:** Throughout New Jersey and Pennsylvania; common along roadsides, woodland edges, old fields, sunny slopes; full to part sun
**Description:** Small shrub or multistemmed tree, up to 30', often forming dense colonies. Compound leaves are alternate, up to 24" long, with 11–31 finely toothed leaflets. Twigs are velvety, densely covered with small hairs. The fruit is an upright cluster of red, fuzzy berries. They may persist on the plant through winter. Leaves turn brilliant red, orange, and purple in the fall.

Staghorn sumac berries make a tart and refreshing summer beverage that goes by the names wild lemonade, sumacade, or rhus juice. It is said to taste like lemonade. I think it has a rich flavor all its own.

Poison sumac. Note the loose hanging cluster of berries, bottom right.

The fuzzy berry clusters are bright red or brownish red and stand upright on the ends of the twigs. The fuzzy twigs resemble deer antlers in velvet. A sumac cluster is sometimes referred to as a "bob."

A lot of people freak out when they hear the word "sumac." During programs where I discuss edible sumac, I very often hear, "I always thought sumac was poisonous." I explain that while there is a poison sumac (*Toxicodendron*

## RECIPE

**Wild Lemonade**

3–4 staghorn sumac clusters
Cold water
Choice of sweetener, if desired

Put the sumac clusters into a quart jar or pitcher. It's OK to push them down and crush them a bit. Pour in water to fill the jar. Let sit for at least 30 minutes, then stick it in the fridge to chill. (***Note:*** Leaving it refrigerated overnight will make it stronger.) Strain before serving. I usually add more water, but you may prefer it good and sour!

*vernix*), it does not produce red berries. Poison sumac berries are whitish, and they hang down. Poison sumac leaves have smooth edges; staghorn sumac leaves are serrated.

All sumac species with red berries are edible and can be used interchangeably. Staghorn sumac is the most common in our area. Smooth sumac (*R. glabra*) has hairless stems, and dwarf sumac (*R. copallina*) has winged leaf stalks.

Sumac berries are used in a tangy spice mix called za'atar, one of most popular condiments in the Middle East. It is made by grinding sumac berries with other spices such as thyme, oregano, and sesame seeds.

To harvest sumac, use clippers to remove the cluster from the plant. You can snap it off by hand, but this is not always easy. In the field, taste a berry or two from each cluster—some will have surprisingly little flavor, while others will be tart. You cannot rely on color as an indicator. The natural acids that give sumac it's lemony flavor are washed away by rain, and the plant will eventually produce more of it. The bobs can be stored for winter in a paper bag kept in a dry place.

Making wild lemonade is simple. It requires only sumac berries and cold water. Hot water will release bitter tannins and change the taste of your drink. Some people prefer to strain the lemonade through a fine sieve to filter out any fine hairs that may irritate the throat. Wild lemonade has a lovely, natural

Sumac clusters can be removed by hand or with clippers.

Wild lemonade is super easy to make!

pinkish color. Enjoy it straight or sweetened to your liking. Mix with seltzer for a nice carbonated beverage.

Staghorn sumac is an excellent source of antioxidants and has appreciable amounts of magnesium (871 mg / kg) and iron (180 mg / kg), as well as an array of B vitamins and vitamin C.

Wintergreen leaf edges have tiny teeth.

## WINTERGREEN
*Gaultheria procumbens*

**Family:** Ericaceae
**Also called:** Checkerberry, teaberry, boxberry
**Uses:** Berries eaten out of hand; leaves and berries for tea
**Cautions:** Avoid if allergic to aspirin.
**Season:** Year-round
**Range:** Throughout New Jersey and Pennsylvania; lightly shaded woodlands
**Description:** A tiny shrub of the forest floor, 3"–5" high, multiple woody stems. Leaf edges have tiny teeth. Crushed leaves release a wintergreen fragrance. Small, white to pink flowers, 5 petals joined into a bell shape, bloom early to midsummer. Berries red, ¼"–⅓".

Although they are not juicy, wintergreen berries are a fun trail nibble. Think of them as wild breath mints. If you've ever tasted teaberry chewing gum or chewed wintergreen candies, you'll recognize the flavor of this plant. The young leaves can be eaten and make a nice salad addition. An interesting batch of muffins can be had by adding a handful of the wintergreen berries to the batter.

**Teaberry Flavoring Extract**

(Use to flavor baked goods or ice cream, as you would vanilla extract.)
1 cup wintergreen leaves
About 1 cup vodka or rum

Roughly chop the leaves. Put them in a 16-ounce jar. Cover with the alcohol; the leaves should be completely submerged. Secure the lid. Let the jar to sit in a dark place for at least 6 weeks, shaking every few days. Strain and pour into a glass bottle. Store in a cool dark place.

The unique flavor of wintergreen, or teaberry, has long held a special place in the culinary traditions of Pennsylvania. The indigenous fruit inspired the creation of Clark's teaberry chewing gum, which originated in Pittsburgh in 1900.

And then there's teaberry ice cream, originally made from the wintergreen plant. It's very much a Pennsylvania thing. Although most recipes nowadays use

Wintergreen, the original flavoring for teaberry ice cream

Wintergreen leaves often turn purple with cold weather.

artificial wintergreen flavoring, the bubble gum–pink ice cream is still a favorite in the Keystone State.

Wintergreen leaves have traditionally been used for tea, hence the common name teaberry. Wintergreen tea was a popular beverage during the Revolutionary War, when regular black tea was unavailable.

Many commercial products have been flavored with natural wintergreen or its synthesized counterpart, including toothpaste, chewing gum (teaberry gum), and breath mints. The wintergreen plant was the original source of wintergreen flavoring. The flavor comes from a chemical called methyl salicylate. The same wintergreen flavor is found in the twigs of black birch (*Betula lenta*), although the two plants are unrelated. Chew on a twig of a birch and see!

Methyl salicylate has a number of modern medicinal applications. In its highly concentrated form, methyl salicylate (also called oil of wintergreen) is widely used in sports creams and other topical pain relievers. When rubbed on the skin, these products act as counterirritants, reducing underlying pain.

While normal food uses of the plant are quite safe, concentrated oil of wintergreen (natural or synthetic) can be toxic. Rare instances of toxicity have been reported from topical application. Methyl salicylate is closely related to aspirin, so don't use wintergreen if you are allergic to aspirin.

Wintergreen leaves and berries have a long history of use in traditional medicine. The plant has been used to treat aches, pains, fever, sore throat, and other maladies. Research shows that the leaves contain significant levels of antioxidants, which may support the plant's use for inflammation. Antioxidant levels in the leaves tend to be greatest in the fall.

Wintergreen also contains the compound gaultherin, which releases salicylates in a time-release fashion, and studies point to wintergreen's potential as a safer aspirin substitute.

Partridge berry, a look-alike plant, often grows near wintergreen. Both are low to the ground, with evergreen leaves and red berries, and both are edible.

Wintergreen berries persist through winter and are eaten by squirrels, chipmunks, deer, and turkeys. The leaves often turn purple with cold weather.

# Mushrooms

Chanterelles may grow in small clusters.

## CHANTERELLES
*Cantharellus* spp.

**Family:** Cantharellaceae
**Also called:** Girolle, true chanterelle, chants
**Uses:** Cap and stem, cooked
**Cautions:** Toxic look-alike. Cook before eating.
**Season:** Summer to fall
**Range:** Throughout New Jersey and Pennsylvania; in mature forests, on the ground under trees, singly or scattered
**Description:** Height 3"–4", cap 2"–4" across. Convex or funnel-shaped cap with wavy irregular edges, usually yellow to orange. Forked cross-veined ridges on cap underside, decurrent. Ridges are firmly attached. Stem not hollow. Flesh is whitish. Stem has no signs of a ring or bulb around the base. Fruity, apricot-like smell. (See below for more details.)

Possibly the most beloved mushroom of all, chanterelles are prized by foragers and gourmet chefs around the world. The various species are highly sought after wherever they grow. All true chanterelles are edible. In addition to their beautiful coloration, chanterelles have a delicate texture and distinctive flavor. They are

Blunt-edged ridges of a golden chanterelle. Note how they fork.

often described as tasting fruity or apricot-like, and mildly peppery. The texture is a melt-in-your-mouth experience.

Chanterelles grow from the ground, singly, scattered, or in small groupings. I have found them in clusters of three, four, and five.

You won't find them growing on dead trees or logs. Chanterelles are mycorrhizal, meaning they form an underground network of fine threads that connect with tree roots. Chanterelles can often be found growing in association with pine, oak, maple, beech, birch, and poplar trees.

On the underside of the chanterelle cap you'll find blunt-edged folds or ridges, sometimes called false gills. They are not sharp-edged gills. The ridges run down the stem and are the same color as the rest of the mushroom. Check for firmly attached ridges that cannot be easily separated or picked off from the cap. The ridges are made from wrinkles or folds in the mushroom; they are not separate structures.

One common variety, the smooth chanterelle (*C. lateritius*), will have fewer or no ridges, or just shallow wrinkles. Golden and smooth chanterelles can look very much alike. They are equally tasty.

The apricot-like smell of chanterelles may be faint if you have only

Smooth chanterelle has fewer ridges on the cap underside.

**Sautéed Chanterelles**

Bring a large skillet to medium-high heat. Add about 1 tablespoon butter or oil. When hot, add the chanterelles. Cook for 5–10 minutes. They will release their liquid. Cook until most of the liquid evaporates and serve. Uneaten portions can be stored in freezer bags. Defrost and use in recipes as needed. Great added to pasta dishes.

one, but when you stick your nose into a bagful of them, the heady scent becomes apparent. When cut open, chanterelle flesh will be whitish. When torn vertically, the flesh is somewhat fibrous and is said to resemble string cheese.

People have mistakenly eaten toxic jack-o'-lantern mushrooms (*Omphalotus illudens*), believing they were chanterelles. Eating a jack-o'-lantern will make you sick with vomiting, cramps, and diarrhea. The two mushrooms have similar coloring, but there are definite ways to tell them apart. The jack-o'-lantern mushroom has true, sharp gills that are unforked. It rarely grows singly. You'll usually find jack-o'-lanterns growing in clumps of a dozen or more, connected at the base. When cut, they are a solid yellowish-orange color inside, and the flesh does not resemble string cheese. They do not have a fruity or apricot-like aroma. Jack-o'-lanterns grow on wood. They may appear to grow from the ground if there is buried wood.

Toxic jack-o'-lantern mushroom. Note the sharp-edged gills and bright orange coloration.

Jack-o'-lantern mushrooms usually grow in clumps of a dozen or more.

After harvest, clean by rinsing under running water while brushing away any visible soil or debris. Chanterelles should always be cooked. Preserve them by cooking first then freezing, or by pickling. They do not dry well for storage.

Black trumpet mushrooms have excellent flavor.

The black trumpet mushroom (*Craterellus fallax*) is another member of the chanterelle family and also a choice edible. Also called horn of plenty, they are a dark brown-black color and can be difficult to see among fallen dried leaves. They look similar to smooth chanterelles except for the color, and also appear in summer and fall.

Black trumpets, also called horn of plenty, are a choice edible mushroom.

Unlike its orange cousins, black trumpets can be dried to preserve their excellent flavor for year-round use. When rehydrated they can be used in a variety of dishes. The flavor is described as smoky or woody, some say reminiscent of truffles.

Chanterelles are a good source of vitamin D and have antioxidant, anti-inflammatory, and antimicrobial properties. Analysis of golden chanterelles shows they are rich in potassium, calcium, zinc, and magnesium. Black trumpets and golden chanterelles have been found to contain considerable levels of vitamin B12, a nutrient obtained almost exclusively from animal sources. It is not clear if these mushrooms have the ability to make B12 or if it is synthesized by bacteria on the mushroom surface.

Chicken mushrooms are one of the easier mushrooms to spot in the woods.

# CHICKEN OF THE WOODS
## *Laetiporus sulphureus*

**Family:** Polyporaceae
**Also called:** Chicken mushroom, sulphur shelf, sulphur polypore, chicken polypore
**Uses:** Tender parts, cooked
**Cautions:** Cook thoroughly and enjoy in moderation. Positive ID as always.
**Season:** Summer, fall
**Range:** Throughout New Jersey and Pennsylvania; on dead or dying hardwood trees, usually oaks
**Description:** Shelf mushroom growing in overlapping clusters on standing trees or fallen trunks. Some specimens over 50 pounds with caps 12" or more across. The brackets are fleshy, yellow to orange on top; color is usually lighter near the edges. A polypore species with tiny pores underneath instead of gills. The pore surface is sulfur-yellow. The mushrooms are knobby when small and young, expanding to fan-shaped, semicircular, or irregular shelves. When young, the flesh is juicy, and will exude a clear or yellowish liquid when cut.

Bright orange clusters of chicken mushrooms are quite easy to spot, even from a distance. They are a good mushroom for beginning foragers, being one of the easier wild mushrooms to identify. But you still need to be careful. The tops of

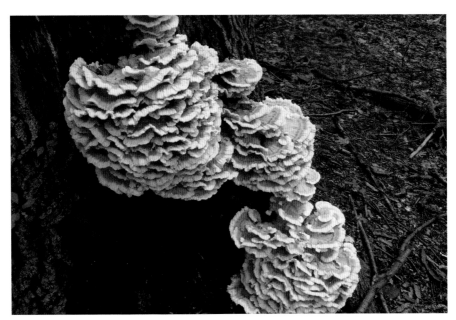
Beautiful ruffled tiers of chicken of the woods

the brackets will display lovely shades of orange and yellow. Check underneath for tiny pores, not gills. Considered a prime edible, these mushrooms have a taste and texture somewhat similar to chicken.

Chicken mushrooms can be substituted in any recipe that calls for chicken. They're good as a simple side dish, in omelets, as main dishes, or breaded and fried as "chicken" cutlets or nuggets.

To harvest chicken mushrooms, cut them off with a knife. Take only fresh, moist specimens; old ones become dry and tough, and can also get buggy. Tough mushrooms can be simmered to make stock. You can harvest the tender outer edges of older caps.

To prepare, remove any soiled or tough areas. Rinse the mushrooms and pat dry. Always thoroughly cook the mushrooms to prevent digestive upset. All it takes is a simple sauté, cooking them in a little butter or olive oil and adding some broth or water as needed to moisten.

Chicken mushrooms have a long history of use as food and herbal medicine in Asia. They are a good

Chicken of the woods, washed and ready to be cut up and cooked

## RECIPE

**Vegetarian "Chicken" Soup**

¼ cup olive oil
2 carrots, sliced
4 stalks celery, sliced
1 medium onion, chopped
4 garlic cloves, chopped
½ pound chicken mushrooms, in thin strips or pieces
8 cups broth
1 bay leaf
2 teaspoons mixed herbs (thyme, basil, oregano, rosemary)
½ pound egg noodles
Salt and pepper to taste

In a large pot, heat the oil over medium heat. Add the carrots, celery, onion, and garlic. Cook until the onion is softened. Stir in the mushrooms, broth, and herbs. Bring to a boil, then reduce heat and simmer for 20 minutes. Add noodles and cook until tender. Adjust seasonings to taste.

"Chicken" noodle soup. Chicken mushrooms are great in soup.

Young, tender chicken of the woods, perfect for harvesting

source of vitamins E and D and B vitamins. Significant amounts of iron, zinc, magnesium, and calcium have been found, with levels varying depending on where the mushrooms were collected. Extracts of *L. sulphureus* have shown antioxidant, antimicrobial, and antitumor activities.

Another species of chicken mushroom, less common in our area, is the white-pored chicken of the woods (*L. cincinnatus*). It looks similar to orange chicken of the woods, but with a white pore surface. It is just as edible.

There are occasional reports of gastric upset and other reactions when consuming chicken mushrooms. This may be due to individual intolerance, improper cooking, or eating the wrong species. Species that grow on eucalyptus, eastern hemlock, and other conifers may be more likely to cause issues. To avoid any intolerance issues, chicken mushrooms should be eaten in moderation. As always, it is advised to eat only a small sample first whenever you try any new food.

To preserve chicken mushrooms for future use, sauté first then freeze them. They do not dry well.

Giant puffballs are a prime edible mushroom species.

## GIANT PUFFBALL
*Calvatia gigantea*

**Family:** Agaricaceae
**Also called:** *Langermannia gigantea* (old name)
**Uses:** Mushroom flesh
**Cautions:** Poisonous look-alikes with smaller specimens (see below).
**Season:** Summer, fall
**Range:** Throughout New Jersey and Pennsylvania; grassy fields, meadows, parks, lawns, open deciduous woods
**Description:** Very large white mushroom, typically at least 1' across. Can grow to 3' in diameter or larger, weighing 50 pounds or more. Shape is more or less round. Inside flesh is pure white, turning yellow or greenish brown when mature (no longer edible). Lacks gills. Lacks a stem and has a thread-like attachment to the ground. May have shallow craters on the surface.

A giant puffball is one of the easiest mushrooms to identify. It bears an uncanny resemblance to a volleyball, especially when sitting on a grassy lawn. Its physical appearance makes this species hard to mistake for any other.

The giant puffball is a prime edible. These huge mushrooms can be cut up and used in any recipe that calls for mushrooms. A typical method of preparation is to simply slice and sauté, maybe with a little garlic or other seasoning. They also make great mushroom soup. The flavor of giant puffball is very mild, and the texture is soft and spongy, often likened to tofu.

When you find a giant puffball, harvesting it is as simple as lifting it from the ground. It is attached to the ground by a cord-like root, which should be cut away, along with any parts that contain embedded dirt.

To make sure your mushroom is safe to eat, you need to check to see that it is the right species, and that it is the right stage for eating. To do this, cut the mushroom in half from top to bottom and examine the inside. It should be pure white with no markings or other colors at all, and especially no sign of gills. If there are gills inside, it means you have another species and it could be quite poisonous. If the flesh is starting to show any color besides pure solid white, it means that

Giant puffballs are easy to harvest. Simply lift them from the ground.

spores are forming, and your puffball should be discarded. A good one should look like marshmallow inside.

## RECIPE

**Puffball Mushroom Soup**

4 tablespoons butter
4 cups chopped mushrooms
1–2 potatoes, chopped (peeled or not)
1 large onion, chopped
¼ cup flour
1 quart broth
1 cup cream
Seasonings to taste: salt, white pepper (recommended), sage, thyme, and a touch of nutmeg

Melt 2 tablespoons of the butter in a large pot over medium-high heat. Sauté the mushrooms, potatoes, and onion for about 5 minutes, until soft. Mix in the flour until smooth. Gradually stir in the broth. Cook, stirring, 5 minutes, or until thick and bubbly. Reduce heat and stir in the cream. Heat through—do not boil. Mix in remaining butter. Season to taste. *Optional:* Blend part or all of the soup with an immersion blender.

A giant puffball, waiting to be cut in half

Giant puffballs have a thin, tender outer skin, which is considered edible but said to cause stomach upset in some individuals. My advice is to remove it. It is easily peeled.

These mushrooms should be eaten soon after harvest, as the quality deteriorates quickly. They will keep for a few days when refrigerated. Due to their enormous size, it is easy to wind up with more than you can fit in your refrigerator. To preserve, sauté then freeze, or use in other cooked dishes that can then be frozen. Freezing raw results in loss of quality.

Giant puffballs also dehydrate well for later use. Slice thinly, process in a dehydrator until completely dry, and store in an airtight container. They can then be used in soups and other dishes. The Iroquois people ate giant puffball mushrooms, especially in soups.

The spores of giant puffballs have been used in Europe and North America as a styptic to stop bleeding and to help with wound healing. Large specimens of *C. gigantea* have been found to produce 5 to 7 trillion spores.

Many lab studies have shown that giant puffball mushrooms have antitumor and antiviral properties. A substance called calvacin, isolated from *C. gigantea,* is a potent antitumor agent. Research suggests that extracts of the mushroom may hold promise in the treatment of lung cancer, either alone or in combination with other drugs.

To harvest your hen, cut it free with a knife.

## HEN OF THE WOODS
*Grifola frondosa*

**Family:** Polyporaceae
**Also called:** *Polyporus frondosus*, hen, *maitake*, sheepshead, king of mushrooms, dancing mushroom
**Uses:** Mushroom, cooked
**Cautions:** No look-alikes of concern
**Season:** Fall
**Range:** Throughout New Jersey and Pennsylvania; trailsides, parks, hardwood forests
**Description:** A large polypore mushroom; grows as a cluster of caps at the base of mature hardwood trees, usually oaks. Can appear like a pile of old leaves at the base of a tree. Each mushroom is usually 1' or more across, and can easily weigh more than 5 pounds. Large specimens can be 50 pounds or more. Caps are thin, fleshy, overlapping, brownish or grayish, and fan-shaped. Cap is up to 3" across, with a short white stem attaching it to the thick mushroom base. Pore surface on the cap underside is white.

Hen of the woods is known as *maitake* in Japan. *Maitake* (pronounced my-TAH-key) means "dancing mushroom" in Japanese, and people are said to dance with

A small hen of the woods cluster. They come in various shades of gray and brown.

joy upon finding the treasured fungus. It has been eaten for thousands of years in Japan and China, where it is valued as both food and medicine. A choice edible mushroom with a rich and woodsy flavor, it has been gaining attention in the United States in recent decades.

Hen of the woods really likes old oak trees. A large tree can have many clusters nestled around its base. Start looking for it in early fall. And remember, they often come back year after year in the same spot.

To remove a hen of the woods mushroom, cut it at the base with a large knife. Brush or cut off as much soil and debris as possible, then bring it home to finish cleaning.

Cut the mushroom through the core into manageable sizes. It should be washed; after all, it has been sitting at the base of a tree. Finish cleaning or trimming away dirt, and cut into smaller sections for cooking or storing.

A nice thing about hen is that it can be frozen without precooking or blanching. Just portion out raw pieces into freezer bags; they should be good for a year.

## RECIPE

**Hen and Egg Skillet (a wild omelet)**

1 tablespoon olive oil
1 tablespoon butter
1 good handful of hen of the woods, in smallish pieces
1 clove garlic (or a few wild garlic bulbs), minced
2 eggs, beaten
Salt and pepper to taste

Heat the oil and butter in a nonstick skillet over medium heat. When hot, add the hen. Cook until tender, about 5 minutes. Add the garlic and cook for another minute. Pour beaten eggs over. When the egg is firm and no longer runny, use a spatula to fold the omelet in half. Heat for another minute or so. Slide the omelet onto a plate, and season to taste.

The caps or thin pieces can be dried in a dehydrator for future use. Rehydrate as needed, and add along with the soaking liquid to soups or sauces. You can reserve the liquid and drink it as a nutrient-rich tea. Add hen pieces to stir-fries, noodles, or rice dishes to lend a chewy texture and earthy flavor. This mushroom is sometimes eaten raw, but cooking may improve its digestibility.

Hen of the woods contains the natural antioxidant compounds ascorbic acid, beta-carotene, tocopherols, phenols, and flavonoids, substances that help protect the body from disease.

Studies over the past thirty years show that *maitake* polysaccharides demonstrate a number of promising bioactivities, including antitumor and antihypertensive properties. *Maitake* contains substances that may help control blood sugar levels in type 2 diabetic patients.

There are no problematic look-alikes for this delicious and healthful mushroom. The black staining polypore (*Meripilus sumstinei*) has a similar appearance and is safe to eat. It stains black when bruised and when cooked. Another edible look-alike, the umbrella polypore (*Polyporus umbellatus*), is lighter in color and is rare in this area.

Hens often come back year after year, so remember your spots.

Hen of the woods is delicious sautéed with onions and peppers.

Lion's mane mushrooms grow on old trees or dead wood.

## LION'S MANE
*Hericium erinaceus*

**Family:** Hericiaceae
**Also called:** Bearded tooth, pompom mushroom
**Uses:** Cooked mushroom
**Cautions:** Look-alikes are not problematic. Those with mushroom allergies should avoid.
**Season:** Fall, early winter
**Range:** Throughout New Jersey and Pennsylvania; on old or dead hardwood trees
**Description:** Rounded, unbranched fruiting body. Does not have a cap. Consists of a clump of hanging white spines that look like little icicles. White, turning yellow or brown with age. When mature, the spines are generally more than ⅓" long.

Lion's mane mushroom doesn't look like your typical mushroom. Instead of a classic cap and stem, this mushroom consists of a clump of hanging teeth, or spines. In addition to its intriguing appearance, lion's mane is a choice edible mushroom. The flavor is frequently compared to crabmeat or lobster.

Lion's mane can sometimes be pretty high up in a tree. Look for a white roundish blob against dark tree bark. It is easily removed from where it's growing.

You probably won't need a knife, but you may need a ladder.

If the lion you find is older and starting to turn yellow, it may still be good to eat. Cut it open and check the flesh: If it's still white inside, it's good.

To prepare your mushroom, rinse out dirt or debris under cool running water, or swish the mushroom in a bowl of water. Drain on towels. Lion's mane is a sturdy mushroom, so don't be afraid to squeeze the water out. Cut into slices or chunks, and cook as you would other mushrooms.

Lion's mane mushroom with icicle-like spines.

Lion's mane mushroom is nutritious. Analysis reveals a dry weight content of 22 percent protein and 57 percent carbohydrate. It is also considered a medicinal mushroom. In China and Japan it has traditionally been used as an anticancer drug and is also used to promote digestion, spleen health, and general strength and vigor.

A very young lion's mane. The spines have not yet fully developed.

Studies have demonstrated that lion's mane improves cognitive function. The mushroom contains hericenones and erinacines, compounds that can stimulate brain cell growth. A double-blind, placebo-controlled trial showed that powdered lion's mane mushroom given orally was effective in improving mild cognitive impairment. The group receiving the lion's mane scored significantly higher on the cognitive function scale. After the study ended and the lion's mane

A large lion's mane harvested from a silver maple tree

supplementation stopped, the scores decreased significantly.

Lion's mane is a beginner-friendly mushroom for foragers. There are no poisonous look-alikes.

**Lion's Mane Medallions**

Lion's mane mushrooms, cut ½ inch thick (enough for one layer in the pan)
1 tablespoon butter
1–2 cloves garlic, minced

Heat a large skillet on medium. Place the mushroom pieces in the dry skillet to remove some of the excess water first. Cook for a few minutes, then turn each piece. When they have released their water and the edges start to brown, add the butter and garlic. Sauté until golden. Season with salt and pepper as desired. Serve hot or at room temperature.

Related species, the coral tooth (*H. coralloides*) and bear's head (*H. americanum*), may be similar in appearance to lion's mane when young. They can have the same compact appearance of lion's mane, but will later develop branching. They are both edible.

The mushrooms are typically prepared by cutting into pieces and frying or sautéing. This may be the finest way to serve lion's mane, highlighting its meaty lobsterlike texture along with crispy frizzled edges. Larger specimens can be sliced into steaks; we'll call smaller ones medallions. Lion's mane can also be steamed or included in soups.

Lion's mane mushroom is delicious when sautéed.

Large mushrooms can be sliced into steaks.

The coveted morel mushroom

## MORELS
*Morchella* spp.

**Family:** Morchellaceae
**Also called:** Spring mushroom, dry land fish
**Uses:** Cooked mushroom
**Cautions:** Look-alikes; possible intolerance
**Season:** April to May
**Range:** Throughout New Jersey and Pennsylvania
**Description:** Morels grow from the ground. The cap is honeycomb-like with pits and ridges. The stem is completely hollow from top to bottom. The cap is completely attached to the stem and not hanging free (except *M. punctipes*; see below). The color of morels may be shades of cream, gray, yellow, brown, or almost black.

Morels are the springtime darlings of the mushroom world. They are the most sought-after of mushrooms, prized for a meaty texture and deep, earthy taste. Mycologists don't agree on the exact number of species, but three common groups are generally recognized: black morels, yellow morels, and half-free morels. All are edible.

Yellow morels come in a variety of colors, from gray to yellow, or even dark brown. The honeycomb-like cap will have ridges lighter than the pits. With black morels, the ridges are darker than the pits.

Morels can be found near dead or dying elm, apple, ash, cottonwood, cherry, poplar, sycamore, and tulip trees. They are well camouflaged, blending

A yellow morel

in with dried leaves, pinecones, and forest floor debris. They often grow abundantly in the spring following a previous summer forest fire, for reasons not completely understood.

Half-free morels (*Morchella punctipes*), while perfectly edible, are usually not considered as desirable as yellow and black morels. Some mushroomers don't even consider them to be real morels, but they are. They are more delicate and less meaty. The cap has dark ridges and lighter pits. The stem has little dots, and faint vertical ribbing. When it's cut in half lengthwise, you will see that the cap is not attached at its base to the stalk. It is attached halfway up the cap, hanging like a skirt. Since the bottom half of the cap hangs free, it's called half-free morel. And like other true morels, it is completely hollow inside.

## RECIPE

### Morels in Cream Sauce

1 tablespoon olive oil
About 3 cups morels, large ones halved, smaller ones left whole (should fit in a single layer in skillet)
3 cloves garlic, minced
2 tablespoons butter
⅓ cup white wine
½ cup heavy cream
2 teaspoons minced fresh herbs (thyme, oregano, chives, parsley)
Salt and pepper to taste

Heat oil in a large skillet over medium-high heat. When hot, add the morels. Cook, stirring occasionally, until they start to brown. Reduce heat to medium. Add the garlic and cook a minute or two. Add the butter and wine. Simmer a few minutes. Add the heavy cream and herbs. Simmer until thickened, at least 5 minutes. Season with salt and pepper. Serve on toast or with pasta.

Half-free morels are true morels. They are small, delicate, and perfectly edible.

There is a group of mushrooms known as "false morels." They are not morels. They are species in the genus *Gyromitra* and are toxic to varying degrees. They should not be eaten. This mushroom bears only a superficial resemblance to morels, but it is still worth mentioning. False morels are short and squat, and the cap is often described as looking brain-like, not honeycomb-like. They are typically reddish brown, sometimes yellowish brown. When cut open, they are not

The half-free morel cap has dark ridges and lighter pits.

Half-free morel. Note the hanging cap and ribbing on the stem.

completely hollow. This is an important distinction—true morels will always be completely hollow inside.

Another group of mushrooms to be aware of belong to the genus *Verpa*. *Verpa* caps resemble a thimble or a bell. The cap is wrinkled, and it hangs completely free from the stem, attached only at the very top of the stem. Controversy surrounds the edibility of *Verpa* mushrooms. Some field guides say they can cause gastrointestinal upset. *V. bohemica* has a long history of being eaten in

All true morels are completely hollow inside.

Italy. It may be a matter of geographic differences, how well the mushrooms are cooked, how much is eaten, or some other factor. My advice: Don't risk it.

To harvest morels, use a knife to cut the stalk near the ground. Cut your mushroom in half from top to bottom. It should be completely hollow. Pick only fresh specimens. Always cook well. Try a small amount the first time to check for any intolerance, and always eat in moderation.

Cleaning morels is important to remove any dirt or bugs. There are many recommendations on how to do this. Cut the mushrooms in half, then either rinse or soak in a bowl of water. Some people soak them overnight, and some recommend using salt water.

Morels are nutritious. Analysis of *M. esculenta* reveals a wide range of nutrients, including protein, ascorbic acid, vitamin D, tocopherols, and carotenoids. Morels also contain compounds with antioxidant, antimicrobial, antiallergenic, anti-inflammatory, and antitumor properties.

Young pheasant's back mushroom with distinctive pattern of brown flecks

## PHEASANT'S BACK
*Polyporus squamosus*

**Family:** Polyporaceae

**Also called:** *Cerioporus squamosus* (newer name), dryad's saddle

**Uses:** Tender portions of caps

**Cautions:** No problematic look-alikes

**Season:** April through June; lesser degree in autumn

**Range:** Throughout New Jersey and Pennsylvania; on decaying stumps and logs, usually elm; occasionally on living trees. They do not grow from the ground.

**Description:** A bracket fungus. Cap is 2"–12" across, fan- or saddle-shaped. They are pale yellow or whitish, with an attractive pattern of brown flecks said to resemble the feathers on a pheasant's back. Caps of older mushrooms lose brown coloring, often fading to white except for a dark blotch in the middle. Caps grow singly or in stacked or overlapping clusters. Pores beneath are white or yellowish, relatively large, and angular. The pore surface extends down the stem. Spores are white. The stem is thick, up to 2" long, and lateral or off-center. Stem is whitish, dark near the base, and it darkens with age.

Pheasant's back is a strikingly beautiful mushroom. Nothing else looks quite like it. Another unique aspect is its aroma, which is said to resemble cucumber or watermelon rind. To my nose, it's always strongly cucumber. It's definitely not a mushroomy smell.

**Braised Pheasant's Back**

1 tablespoon olive oil
1 tablespoon butter
2–3 small pheasant's back mushroom caps, thinly sliced
Fresh lemon juice
Salt and pepper

Heat a large skillet over medium heat. Add the oil and butter. When hot, add the mushrooms. Sauté until they start to brown a bit. This may take 5 minutes or longer. Taste a piece; if nice and tender, sprinkle with lemon juice, a bit of salt and pepper, and enjoy. If a more tender texture is desired, add a little broth or water and continue cooking. Cook until the liquid is evaporated and the mushrooms are tender.

Despite the fact that it is a very edible species, pheasant's back doesn't seem to have a very big following. Some people don't appreciate the smell. Others compare it unfavorably to the morels they were really looking for, sometimes complaining that they "only" found pheasant's backs. The two mushrooms share the same season.

Pheasant's back is an especially good species for beginners. The eye-catching mushroom has no poisonous look-alikes. It is plentiful during spring and easily

Pheasant's back mushroom has a cucumber-like aroma.

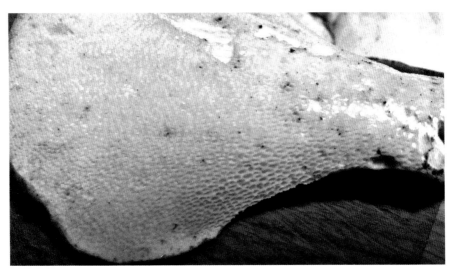

Pores on the underside of a pheasant's back cap

identifiable. Always look for the unique cap markings and the pores underneath. And check the smell while you're at it.

Pheasant's backs tend to grow back in the same spot year after year. When harvesting, focus on the smaller caps. About 2–4 inches across is perfect; after that they start to get tough. Larger and tougher mushrooms may still have tender edges, which can be trimmed off and used.

Pheasant's back, also known as dryad's saddle, can have saddle-shaped caps.

The flavor of cooked pheasant's back is mild and mushroomy. You may still detect a hint of that cucumber-like essence after cooking. To prepare, wash the caps under running water then drain them pore-side down on towels. Squeeze to dry. Slice thinly, or cut into small chunks. Set aside stems and tougher parts for later use; a long simmer will turn these into a nourishing stock.

Pheasant's back mushrooms are nutritious. They have an assortment of nutrients and are protein-rich, although exact composition of nutrients varies among studies. This may be related to different conditions, such as soil and climate. The mushrooms contain 385 calories per 100 g (3½ ounces) dry weight.

Pheasant's back has been shown in laboratory studies to have anticancer and immunomodulatory properties. Extracts demonstrate positive effects on the immune system and are thought to hold promise in the treatment of intestinal tract disorders. Studies also show that extracts of *P. squamosus* possess antioxidant and antimicrobial properties. Activity was especially high against *Staphylococcus aureus*, or "staph" bacteria.

# BIBLIOGRAPHY

**Plants of Spring**

*Black Locust* (**Robinia pseudoacacia**)

Stankov, Stanko, Hafize Fidan, Tanya Ivanova, Albena Stoyanova, Stanka Damyanova, and Mykola Desyk. "Chemical Composition and Application of Flowers of False Acacia (*Robinia Pseudoacacia* L.)." *Ukrainian Food Journal* 7, no. 4 (2018): 577–88. https://doi.org/10.24263/2304-974x-2018-7-4-4.

*Cattail* (**Typha** *spp.*)

Harris, Ben Charles. *Eat the Weeds*. Barre, MA: Barre Publishers, 1969.

Phillips, Katherine M., Pamela R. Pehrsson, Wanda W. Agnew, Angela J. Scheett, Jennifer R. Follett, Henry C. Lukaski, and Kristine Y. Patterson. "Nutrient Composition of Selected Traditional United States Northern Plains Native American Plant Foods." *Journal of Food Composition and Analysis* 34, no. 2 (June 2014): 136–52. https://doi.org/10.1016/j .jfca.2014.02.010.

*Chickweed* (**Stellaria media**)

*Cerastium arvense* var. *villosissimum*. New York Botanical Garden. http:// navigator.nybg.org/weboi/oecgi2.exe/INET_ECM_DispPl?NAMENUM=1 2103&DETAIL=1&startpage=1.

Chidrawar, Vijayr, Sunilb Bothra, Akshayr Koli, Krishnakantn Patel, Shrutis Shiromwar, and Gajanang Kalyankar. "Anti-Obesity Effect of Stellaria Media Methanolic Extract in the Murine Model of Cafeteria Diet Induced Obesity." *International Journal of Nutrition, Pharmacology, Neurological Diseases* 2, no. 2 (2012): 121. https://doi.org/10.4103/2231-0738.95963.

Stark, Philip B., Daphne Miller, Thomas J. Carlson, and Kristen Rasmussen De Vasquez. "Open-Source Food: Nutrition, Toxicology, and Availability of Wild Edible Greens in the East Bay." *Plos One* 14, no. 1 (2019). https://doi .org/10.1371/journal.pone.0202450.

### *Chicory* (**Cichorium intybus**)

Bowes, Anna de Planter, Jean A. T. Pennington, and Helen Nichols Church. *Food Values of Portions Commonly Used*. Philadelphia, PA: Lippincott, 1998.

"Chicory Greens, Raw." FoodData Central. USDA Agricultural Research Service. https://fdc.nal.usda.gov.

"Noxious Weeds." Department of Agriculture. Pennsylvania Bulletin. Harrisburg, PA. www.pacodeandbulletin.gov/Display/pabull?file=/secure/pabulletin/data/vol49/49-41/1511.html.

Smith, Andrew, David Sutherland, and Paul Hewlett. "An Investigation of the Acute Effects of Oligofructose-Enriched Inulin on Subjective Wellbeing, Mood and Cognitive Performance." *Nutrients* 7, no. 11 (2015): 8887–96. https://doi.org/10.3390/nu7115441.


### *Cleavers* (**Galium aparine**)

Butnariu, Monica. "Vegetal Metabolomics to Seeds of *Galium Aparine*." *Journal of Bioequivalence & Bioavailability* 05, no. 07 (2013). https://doi.org/10.4172/jbb.10000e45.

Elias, Thomas S., and Peter A. Dykeman. *Edible Wild Plants: A North American Field Guide*. San Bernardino, CA: Borgo Press, 1993.

Krochmal, Arnold, Russell S. Walters, and Richard M. Doughty. *A Guide to Medicinal Plants of Appalachia*. Washington: U.S. Forest Service; for sale by the Supt. of Docs., U.S. Govt. Print. Off., 1971.


### *Curly Dock* (**Rumex crispus**)

"Dock, Raw." FoodData Central. USDA Agricultural Research Service. https://fdc.nal.usda.gov/fdc-app.html#/?query=dock.

Feduraev, Pavel, Galina Chupakhina, Pavel Maslennikov, Natalia Tacenko, and Liubov Skrypnik. "Variation in Phenolic Compounds Content and Antioxidant Activity of Different Plant Organs from *Rumex Crispus* L. and *Rumex Obtusifolius* L. at Different Growth Stages." *Antioxidants* 8, no. 7 (July 23, 2019): 237. https://doi.org/10.3390/antiox8070237.

### Dandelion (Taraxacum officinale)

Cai, Liangliang, Fanglian Yi, Libiao Luan, and Dongwei Wan. "Purification, Preliminary Characterization and Hepatoprotective Effects of Polysaccharides from Dandelion Root." *Molecules* 22, no. 9 (2017): 1409. https://doi.org/10.3390/molecules22091409.

Chatterjee, S. J., P. Ovadje, M. Mousa, C. Hamm, and S. Pandey. "The Efficacy of Dandelion Root Extract in Inducing Apoptosis in Drug-Resistant Human Melanoma Cells." *Evidence-Based Complementary and Alternative Medicine* 2011 (2011): 1–11. https://doi.org/10.1155/2011/129045.

"Dandelion." FoodData Central. USDA Agricultural Research Service. https://fdc.nal.usda.gov/fdc-app.html#/?query=Dandelion.

González-Castejón, Marta, Francesco Visioli, and Arantxa Rodriguez-Casado. "Diverse Biological Activities of Dandelion." *Nutrition Reviews* 70, no. 9 (September 2012): 534–47. https://doi.org/10.1111/j.1753-4887.2012.00509.x.

### Dame's Rocket (Hesperis matronalis)

Francis, A., P. B. Cavers, and S. I. Warwick. "The Biology of Canadian Weeds. 140. *Hesperis Matronalis* L." *Canadian Journal of Plant Science* 89, no. 1 (January 2009): 191–206. https://doi.org/10.4141/cjps08094.

### Eastern White Pine (Pinus strobus)

Anderson, James V., Boris I. Chevone, and John L. Hess. "Seasonal Variation in the Antioxidant System of Eastern White Pine Needles." *Plant Physiology* 98, no. 2 (February 1, 1992): 501–508. https://doi.org/10.1104/pp.98.2.501.

Verhoeven, A., A. Osmolak, P. Morales, and J. Crow. "Seasonal Changes in Abundance and Phosphorylation Status of Photosynthetic Proteins in Eastern White Pine and Balsam Fir." *Tree Physiology* 29, no. 3 (March 19, 2009): 361–74. https://doi.org/10.1093/treephys/tpn031.

### Garlic Mustard (Alliaria petiolata)

Guil-Guerrero, José Luis, Juan José Giménez-Martínez, and María Esperanza Torija-Isasa. "Nutritional Composition of Wild Edible Crucifer Species." *Journal of Food Biochemistry* 23, no. 3 (February 23, 2007): 283–94. https://doi.org/10.1111/j.1745-4514.1999.tb00020.x.

### *Greenbrier* (**Smilax rotundifolia**)

Lu, Chuan-Li, Wei Zhu, Min Wang, Xiao-Jie Xu, and Chuan-Jian Lu. "Antioxidant and Anti-Inflammatory Activities of Phenolic-Enriched Extracts of *Smilax Glabra*." *Evidence-Based Complementary and Alternative Medicine* 2014 (2014): 1–8. https://doi.org/10.1155/2014/910438.

Uphof, J. C. *Dictionary of Economic Plants*. Lehre: Verlag von J. Cramer, 1968.

### *Hairy Bittercress* (**Cardamine hirsuta**)

Konsam, Sanjita Chanu, Kangjam Tilotama Devi, Jekendra Singh Salam, and Potshangbam Kumar Singh. "Biochemical Constituents and Nutritive Evaluation of Some Less Known Wild Edible Plants from Senapati District, Manipur, India." *Notulae Scientia Biologicae* 8, no. 3 (2016): 370–72. https://doi.org/10.15835/nsb839871.

Šircelj, Helena, Maja Mikulic-Petkovsek, Robert Veberič, Metka Hudina, and Ana Slatnar. "Lipophilic Antioxidants in Edible Weeds from Agricultural Areas." *Turkish Journal of Agriculture and Forestry* 42 (2018): 1–10. https://doi.org/10.3906/tar-1707-25.

### *Henbit* (**Lamium amplexicaule**)

Fernald, Merritt Lyndon, and Alfred Charles Kinsey. *Edible Wild Plants of Eastern North America*. New York, NY: Harper & Row Publishers, 1943.

Salehi, Bahare, Lorene Armstrong, Antonio Rescigno, Balakyz Yeskaliyeva, Gulnaz Seitimova, Ahmet Beyatli, Jugreet Sharmeen, et al. "Lamium Plants—A Comprehensive Review on Health Benefits and Biological Activities." *Molecules* 24, no. 10 (2019): 1913. https://doi.org/10.3390/molecules24101913.

### *Japanese Knotweed* (**Polygonum cuspidatum**)

Catalgol, Betul, Saime Batirel, Yavuz Taga, and Nesrin Kartal Ozer. "Resveratrol: French Paradox Revisited." *Frontiers in Pharmacology* 3 (July 17, 2012). https://doi.org/10.3389/fphar.2012.00141.

Feng, Jie, Jacob Leone, Sunjya Schweig, and Ying Zhang. "Evaluation of Natural and Botanical Medicines for Activity Against Growing and Non-Growing Forms of *B. Burgdorferi*." *Frontiers in Medicine* 7 (February 21, 2020). https://doi.org/10.3389/fmed.2020.00006.

## *Maple* (**Acer** *spp.*)

Bowes, Anna de Planter, Jean A. T. Pennington, and Helen Nichols Church. *Food Values of Portions Commonly Used*. Philadelphia, PA: Lippincott, 1998.

Taylor, Fred H. *Variation in Sugar Content of Maple Sap*. Burlington, VT: Agricultural Experiment Station, University of Vermont, and State Agricultural College, 1956.

## *Ostrich Fern* (**Matteuccia struthiopteris**)

Delong, John, D. Mark Hodges, Robert Prange, Charles Forney, Peter Toivenon, M. Conny Bishop, Michele Elliot, and Michael Jordan. "The Unique Fatty Acid and Antioxidant Composition of Ostrich Fern (*Matteuccia Struthiopteris*) Fiddleheads." *Canadian Journal of Plant Science* 91, no. 5 (2011): 919–30. https://doi.org/10.4141/cjps2010-042.

Lord, Thomas R., and Holly J. Travis. *The Ferns and Allied Plants of Pennsylvania*. Indiana, PA: Dept. of Biology, Indiana University of Pennsylvania, 2006.

"Ostrich Fern Poisoning—New York and Western Canada, 1994." Centers for Disease Control and Prevention, September 23, 1994. www.cdc.gov/mmwr/preview/mmwrhtml/00032588.htm.

## *Plantain* (**Plantago** *spp.*)

Chiang, Lien-Chai, Lean Teik Ng, Wen Chiang, Mei-Yin Chang, and Chun-Ching Lin. "Immunomodulatory Activities of Flavonoids, Monoterpenoids, Triterpenoids, Iridoid Glycosides and Phenolic Compounds of *Plantago* Species." *Planta Medica* 69, no. 7 (2003): 600–604. https://doi.org/10.1055/s-2003-41113.

Guillén, María Elena Núñez, José Artur Da Silva Emim, Caden Souccar, and Antonio José Lapa. "Analgesic and Anti-Inflammatory Activities of the Aqueous Extract of Plantago Major L." *International Journal of Pharmacognosy* 35, no. 2 (1997): 99–104. https://doi.org/10.1076/phbi.35.2.99.13288.

Hawthorn, Wayne R. "The Biology of Canadian Weeds. 4. *Plantago Major* and *P. Rugelii*." *Canadian Journal of Plant Science* 54, no. 2 (1974): 383–96. https://doi.org/10.4141/cjps74-059.

### *Purple Deadnettle* (**Lamium purpureum**)
Redzic, Sule Jman. "Wild Edible Plants and Their Traditional Use in the Human Nutrition in Bosnia-Herzegovina." *Ecology of Food and Nutrition* 45, no. 3 (2006): 189–232. https://doi.org/10.1080/03670240600648963

### *Ramps* (**Allium tricoccum**)
Lewis, Courtney. "The Case of the Wild Onions: The Impact of Ramps on Cherokee Rights." *Southern Cultures* 18, no. 2 (2012): 104–17. https://doi.org/10.1353/scu.2012.0019.

### *Redbud* (**Cercis canadensis**)
Moerman, Daniel E. *Native American Ethnobotany*. Portland, OR: Timber Press, 2016.

Zennie, Thomas M., and Dwayne Ogzewalla. "Ascorbic Acid and Vitamin A Content of Edible Wild Plants of Ohio and Kentucky." *Economic Botany* 31, no. 1 (January 1977): 76–79. https://doi.org/10.1007/bf02860657.

### *Spring Beauty* (**Claytonia virginica**)
Gibbons, Euell. *Stalking the Wild Asparagus*; with Illus. by Margaret F. Schroeder. New York, NY: D. McKay Co., 1962.

Snyder, David B. "A New Status for New Jersey's Yellow Spring Beauty." *Bartonia*, no. 57 (1992): 39–49. www.jstor.org/stable/44898396.

### *Spruce* (**Picea *spp.***)
Couplan François. *The Encyclopedia of Edible Plants of North America*. New Canaan, CT: Keats Pub., 1998.

Rautio, M., A. Sipponen, R. Peltola, J. Lohi, J. J. Jokinen, A. Papp, P. Carlson, and P. Sipponen. "Antibacterial Effects of Home-Made Resin Salve from Norway Spruce (Picea Abies)." *Apmis* 115, no. 4 (April 2007): 335–40. https://doi.org/10.1111/j.1600-0463.2007.apm_548.x.

Tantaquidgeon, Gladys. *Folk Medicine of the Delaware and Related Algonkian Indians*. Harrisburg, PA: Pennsylvania Historical and Museum Commission, 1972.

*Stinging Nettle* (**Urtica dioica**)

Phillips, Katherine M., Pamela R. Pehrsson, Wanda W. Agnew, Angela J. Scheett, Jennifer R. Follett, Henry C. Lukaski, and Kristine Y. Patterson. "Nutrient Composition of Selected Traditional United States Northern Plains Native American Plant Foods." *Journal of Food Composition and Analysis* 34, no. 2 (June 2014): 136–52. https://doi.org/10.1016/j .jfca.2014.02.010.

Randall, Colin, Hester Randall, Frank Dobbs, Charles Hutton, and Hilary Sanders. "Randomized Controlled Trial of Nettle Sting for Treatment of Base-of-Thumb Pain." *Journal of the Royal Society of Medicine* 93, no. 6 (2000): 305–309. https://doi.org/10.1177/014107680009300607.

Safarinejad, Mohammad Reza. "*Urtica Dioica* for Treatment of Benign Prostatic Hyperplasia." *Journal of Herbal Pharmacotherapy* 5, no. 4 (2006): 1–11. https://doi.org/10.1300/j157v05n04_01.


*Trout Lily* (**Erythronium americanum**)

Foster, Steven, and James A. Duke. *Field Guide to Medicinal Plants and Herbs of Eastern and Central North America.* Boston, MA: Houghton Mifflin Harcourt, 2014.

Vos, Belinda L. "Lamb's Tongue: The *Erythronium* Species of Jackson County, and the Botanists Who Collected and Described Them." *Kalmiopsis* 10 (2003): 11-22. www.npsoregon.org/kalmiopsis/kalmiopsis_v10. pdf#page=13.


*Violets* (**Viola *spp.***)

Toiu, A., L. Vlase, I. Oniga, and M. Tamas. "HPLC Analysis of Salicylic Acid Derivatives from *Viola* Species." *Chemistry of Natural Compounds* 44, no. 3 (2008): 357–58. https://doi.org/10.1007/s10600-008-9060-9.

Zennie, Thomas M., and Dwayne Ogzewalla. "Ascorbic Acid and Vitamin A Content of Edible Wild Plants of Ohio and Kentucky." *Economic Botany* 31, no. 1 (1977): 76–79. https://doi.org/10.1007/bf02860657.


*Wild Garlic* (**Allium vineale**)

Petropoulos, Spyridon A., Francesco Di Gioia, Nikos Polyzos, and Nikos Tzortzakis. "Natural Antioxidants, Health Effects and Bioactive Properties of Wild *Allium* Species." *Current Pharmaceutical Design* 26 (March 2020). https://doi.org/10.2174/1381612826666200203145851.

Satyal, Prabodh, Jonathan D Craft, Noura S Dosoky, and William N Setzer. "The Chemical Compositions of the Volatile Oils of Garlic (*Allium sativum*) and Wild Garlic (*Allium vineale*)." *Foods* 6, no. 8 (August 5, 2017): 63. https://doi.org/10.3390/foods6080063.

### *Wintercress* (Barbarea vulgaris)
Franke, W., and A. Kensbock. "Vitamin C Content of Native Wild Growing Vegetables and Greens." *Ernaehr-Umsch* 28, (1982): 187-191. www .researchgate.net/publication/277262841_Brassicaceae_A_rich_source_of_ health_improving_phytochemicals.

## Plants of Summer

### *Beach Plum* (Prunus maritima)
Bowman's Hill Wildflower Preserve. "Beach Plum (*Prunus maritima*)." 2020. https://bhwp.org/item/beach-plum-prunus-maritima/.

Garrick, Les. "Banking on Beach Plums." *Gastronomica* 12, no. 3 (August 1, 2012): 21–30. https://doi.org/10.1525/gfc.2012.12.3.21.

### *Black Cherry* (Prunus serotina)
Arnason, Thor, Richard J. Hebda, and Timothy Johns. "Use of Plants for Food and Medicine by Native Peoples of Eastern Canada." *Canadian Journal of Botany* 59, no. 11 (January 1981): 2189–2325. https://doi.org/10.1139/ b81-287.

Luna-Vázquez, Francisco, César Ibarra-Alvarado, Alejandra Rojas-Molina, Juana Rojas-Molina, Elhadi Yahia, Dulce Rivera-Pastrana, Adriana Rojas-Molina, and Ángel Miguel Zavala-Sánchez. "Nutraceutical Value of Black Cherry *Prunus Serotina* Ehrh. Fruits: Antioxidant and Antihypertensive Properties." *Molecules* 18, no. 12 (November 25, 2013): 14597–612. https://doi.org/10.3390/molecules181214597.

### *Blueberry* (Vaccinium *spp.*)
Devore, Elizabeth E., Jae Hee Kang, Monique M. B. Breteler, and Francine Grodstein. "Dietary Intakes of Berries and Flavonoids in Relation to Cognitive Decline." *Annals of Neurology* 72, no. 1 (April 26, 2012): 135–43. https://doi.org/10.1002/ana.23594.

Piljac-Žegarac, J., A. Belščak, and A. Piljac. "Antioxidant Capacity and Polyphenolic Content of Blueberry (*Vaccinium Corymbosum* L.) Leaf Infusions." *Journal of Medicinal Food* 12, no. 3 (July 2009): 608–14. https://doi.org/10.1089/jmf.2008.0081.

### *Brambles* (**Rubus** *spp.*)

Bowen-Forbes, Camille S., Yanjun Zhang, and Muraleedharan G. Nair. "Anthocyanin Content, Antioxidant, Anti-Inflammatory and Anticancer Properties of Blackberry and Raspberry Fruits." *Journal of Food Composition and Analysis* 23, no. 6 (2010): 554–60. https://doi.org/10.1016/j.jfca.2009.08.012.

Pantelidis, G., M. Vasilakakis, G. Manganaris, and G. Diamantidis. "Antioxidant Capacity, Phenol, Anthocyanin and Ascorbic Acid Contents in Raspberries, Blackberries, Red Currants, Gooseberries and Cornelian Cherries." *Food Chemistry* 102, no. 3 (2007): 777–83. https://doi.org/10.1016/j.foodchem.2006.06.021.

### *Common Milkweed* (**Asclepias syriaca**)

Gaertner, Erika E. "The History and Use of Milkweed (*Asclepias Syriaca* L.)." *Economic Botany* 33, no. 2 (1979): 119–23. https://doi.org/10.1007/bf02858278.

Kindscher, Kelly, Leanne Martin, Steve Corbett, and David Lafond. "Nutritional Properties of Native Plants and Traditional Foods from the Central United States." *Ethnobiology Letters* 9, no. 2 (April 2018): 214–27. https://doi.org/10.14237/ebl.9.2.2018.1219.

Thayer, Samuel. *The Forager's Harvest: A Guide to Identifying, Harvesting, and Preparing Edible Wild Plants.* Bruce, WI: Forager's Harvest Press, 2006.

### *Cornelian Cherry* (**Cornus mas**)

Czerwińska, Monika E., and Matthias F. Melzig. "*Cornus Mas* and *Cornus Officinalis*—Analogies and Differences of Two Medicinal Plants Traditionally Used." *Frontiers in Pharmacology* 9 (2018). https://doi.org/10.3389/fphar.2018.00894.

### *Elderberry* (**Sambucus canadensis** *and* **S. nigra**)

Torabian, Golnoosh, Peter Valtchev, Qayyum Adil, and Fariba Dehghani. "Anti-Influenza Activity of Elderberry (*Sambucus nigra*)." *Journal of Functional Foods* 54 (2019): 353–60. https://doi.org/10.1016/j.jff.2019.01.031.

### *Heal-All* (**Prunella vulgaris**)

Huang, Mofei, Yian Wang, Ling Xu, and Ming You. "Anti-Tumor Properties of *Prunella Vulgaris*." *Current Pharmacology Reports* 1, no. 6 (May 15, 2015): 401–19. https://doi.org/10.1007/s40495-015-0038-6.

Rasool, Rafia, and Bashir A. Ganai. "*Prunella Vulgaris* L.: A Literature Review on Its Therapeutic Potentials." *Pharmacologia* 4, no. 6 (2013): 441–48. https://doi.org/10.5567/pharmacologia.2013.441.448.

Yanovsky, Elias. USDA. *Food Plants of the North American Indians.* Washington DC: US Government Printing Office, (1936).

Zhao, Jixue, Degang Ji, Xujie Zhai, Lirong Zhang, Xiao Luo, and Xin Fu. "Oral Administration of *Prunella Vulgaris* L Improves the Effect of Taxane on Preventing the Progression of Breast Cancer and Reduces Its Side Effects." *Frontiers in Pharmacology* 9 (August 3, 2018). https://doi.org/10.3389/fphar.2018.00806.

### *Lamb's-quarter* (**Chenopodium album**)

Bowes, Anna de Planter, Jean A. T. Pennington, and Helen Nichols Church. *Food Values of Portions Commonly Used.* Philadelphia, PA: Lippincott, 1998.

Khoobchandani, Menka, B. K. Ojeswi, Bhavna Sharma, and Man Mohan Srivastava. "*Chenopodium album* Prevents Progression of Cell Growth and Enhances Cell Toxicity in Human Breast Cancer Cell Lines." *Oxidative Medicine and Cellular Longevity* 2, no. 3 (2009): 160–65. https://doi.org/10.4161/oxim.2.3.8837.

Poonia, Amrita, and Ashutosh Upadhayay. "*Chenopodium Album* Linn: Review of Nutritive Value and Biological Properties." *Journal of Food Science and Technology* 52, no. 7 (April 7, 2015): 3977–85. https://doi.org/10.1007/s13197-014-1553-x.

### *Mayapple* (**Podophyllum peltatum**)

Fenton, William N. *Contacts between Iroquois Herbalism and Colonial Medicine.* Seattle, WA: Shorey Book Store, 1971.

Pearce, Douglas K., and John W. Thieret. "Persimmon (*Diospyros virginiana*, Ebenaceae) and Mayapple (*Podophyllum peltatum*, Berberidaceae): Proximate Analysis of Their Fruits." Transactions of the Kentucky Academy of Science v.53–55 (1993): 30–31. https://agris.fao.org/agris-search/search.do?recordID=US9420450.

Schwartz, James, and Scott A. Norton. "Useful Plants of Dermatology. VI. The Mayapple (*Podophyllum*)." *Journal of the American Academy of Dermatology* 47, no. 5 (2002): 774–75. https://doi.org/10.1067/mjd.2002.125081.

### *Mulberry* (Morus alba *and* M. rubra)
Bowes, Anna de Planter, Jean A. T. Pennington, and Helen Nichols Church. *Food Values of Portions Commonly Used*. Philadelphia, PA: Lippincott, 1998.

Duke, James A. "Handbook of Energy Crops." Unpublished.

### *Oxeye Daisy* (Leucanthemum vulgare)
Magharri, Elham, Seyed M. Razavi, Erdevan Ghorbani, Lutfun Nahar, and Satyajit D. Sarker. "Chemical Composition, Some Allelopathic Aspects, Free-Radical Scavenging Property and Antifungal Activity of the Volatile Oil of the Flowering Tops of *Leucanthemum vulgare* Lam." *Records of Natural Products* 9:4 (2015): 538–45. https://search.proquest.com/openview/aca4b8aec3d797c64534543d0d3902b5/1?pq-origsite=gscholar&cbl=2042708.

Zennie, Thomas M., and Dwayne Ogzewalla. "Ascorbic Acid and Vitamin A Content of Edible Wild Plants of Ohio and Kentucky." *Economic Botany* 31, no. 1 (1977): 76–79. https://doi.org/10.1007/bf02860657.

### *Purslane* (Portulaca oleracea)
Bowes, Anna de Planter, Jean A. T. Pennington, and Helen Nichols Church. *Food Values of Portions Commonly Used*. Philadelphia, PA: Lippincott, 1998.

Holm, LeRoy G., D. L. Plucknett, J. V. Pancho, and J. P. Herberger. *The World's Worst Weeds: Distribution and Biology*. Malabar, FL: Krieger publ., 1991.

Uddin, M. K., A. S. Juraimi, M. S. Hossain, M. A. U. Nahar, M. E. Ali, and M. M. Rahman (2014). "Purslane Weed (*Portulaca oleracea*): A Prospective Plant Source of Nutrition, Omega-3 Fatty Acid, and Antioxidant Attributes. *The Scientific World Journal*. Scientific World Ltd. https://doi.org/10.1155/2014/951019.

**_Queen Anne's Lace_ (Daucus carota)**

Gibbons, Euell. *Stalking the Healthful Herbs*. New York, NY: McKay Co., 1970.

Jansen, Gabrielle Claire, and Hans Wohlmuth. "Carrot Seed for Contraception: A Review." *Australian Journal of Herbal Medicine* 26, No. 1 (2014):10–17. www.researchgate.net/publication/289343049.

USDA Agricultural Research Service, D. B. Haytowitz, A. L. Eldridge, S. Bhagwat, S. E. Gebhardt, J. M. Holden, G. R. Beecher, J. Peterson, and J. Dwyer. "Flavonoid Content of Vegetables" (2002). www.ars.usda.gov/ARSUserFiles/80400525/Articles/AICR03_VegFlav.pdf.


**_Serviceberry_ (Amelanchier _spp._)**

Donno, D., A. K. Cerutti, M. G. Mellano, Z. Prgomet, and G. l. Beccaro. "Serviceberry, a Berry Fruit with Growing Interest of Industry: Physicochemical and Quali-Quantitative Health-Related Compound Characterisation." *Journal of Functional Foods* 26 (October 2016): 157–66. https://doi.org/10.1016/j.jff.2016.07.014.

Michalczyk, Magdalena, and Ryszard Macura. "Effect of Processing and Storage on the Antioxidant Activity of Frozen and Pasteurized Shadblow Serviceberry (*Amelanchier canadensis*)." *International Journal of Food Properties* 13, no. 6 (2010): 1225–33. https://doi.org/10.1080/10942910903013407.


**_Spearmint_ (Mentha spicata)**

"Spearmint, Fresh." FoodData Central. USDA Agricultural Research Service. April 1, 2019. https://fdc.nal.usda.gov/fdc-app.html#/food-details/173475/nutrients.

Yousuf, Patwary Md Hajjaj, Nusrat Yousuf Noba, Mohammad Shohel, Rajib Bhattacherjee, and Biplab Kumar Das. "Analgesic, Anti-Inflammatory and Antipyretic Effect of *Mentha spicata* (Spearmint)." *British Journal of Pharmaceutical Research* 3, no. 4 (July 18, 2013): 854–64. https://doi.org/10.9734/bjpr/2013/4640.

**Strawberry / Wild Strawberry (Fragaria virginiana)**

Hu, Weicheng, Wei Shen, and Myeong-Hyeon Wang. "Free Radical Scavenging Activity and Protective Ability of Methanolic Extract from *Duchesnea Indica* Against Protein Oxidation and DNA Damage." *Preventive Nutrition and Food Science* 14, no. 4 (2009): 277–82. https://doi.org/10.3746/jfn.2009.14.4.277.

Satterfield, G. Howard, and Mary Yarbrough. "Varietal Differences in Ascorbic Acid (Vitamin C) Content of Strawberries." *Journal of Food Science* 5, no. 3 (1940): 241–45. https://doi.org/10.1111/j.1365-2621.1940.tb17187.x.


**Watercress (Nasturtium officinale)**

Bowes, Anna de Planter, Jean A. T. Pennington, and Helen Nichols Church. *Food Values of Portions Commonly Used*. Philadelphia, PA: Lippincott, 1998.

Di Noia, Jennifer. "Defining Powerhouse Fruits and Vegetables: A Nutrient Density Approach." *Preventing Chronic Disease* 11 (2014). https://doi.org/10.5888/pcd11.130390.

Haro, G., I. Iksen, R. M. Rumanti, N. Marbun, R. P. Sari, and R. P. J. Gultom. "Evaluation of Antioxidant Activity and Minerals Value from Watercress (*Nasturtium Officinale* R.Br.)." *Rasayan Journal of Chemistry* 11 (2018): 232–37. https://doi.org/10.7324/rjc.2018.1112011.


**Wood Sorrel (Oxalis stricta)**

Holmes, Ross P., Harold O. Goodman, and Dean G. Assimos. "Contribution of Dietary Oxalate to Urinary Oxalate Excretion." *Kidney International* 59, no. 1 (January 2001): 270–76. https://doi.org/10.1046/j.1523-1755.2001.00488.x.

Shad, A. A., H. U. Shah, and J. Bakht. "Ethnobotanical Assessment and Nutritive Potential of Wild Food Plants." *Journal of Animal and Plant Sciences* 23(1) (2013): 92–97. https://pdfs.semanticscholar.org/213a/bb7a1 3ef2d428dab6b14f3e01b3073cd167f.pdf.

## Plants of Fall

### *Autumn Olive* (**Elaeagnus umbellata**)

Khanzadi, Fatima Khattak. "Free Radical Scavenging Activity, Phytochemical Composition and Nutrient Analysis of *Elaeagnus Umbellata* Berry." *Journal of Medicinal Plants Research* 6, no. 39 (October 10, 2012): 5196–5203. https://doi.org/10.5897/jmpr11.1128.

### *Beech* (**Fagus grandifolia**)

Hamel, Paul B., and Mary U. Chiltoskey. *Cherokee Plants and Their Uses: A 400 Year History.* Sylva, NC: Herald Publishing, 1975.

"Nuts, Beechnuts, Dried." FoodData Central. USDA Agricultural Research Service. https://fdc.nal.usda.gov/fdc-app.html#/food-details/170161/nutrients.

### *Black Walnut* (**Juglans nigra**)

"Nuts, Walnuts, Black, Dried." FoodData Central. USDA Agricultural Research Service. https://fdc.nal.usda.gov.

Sánchez-González, Claudia, Carlos J. Ciudad, Véronique Noé, and Maria Izquierdo-Pulido. "Health Benefits of Walnut Polyphenols: An Exploration beyond Their Lipid Profile." *Critical Reviews in Food Science and Nutrition* 57, no. 16 (December 29, 2015): 3373–83. https://doi.org/10.1080/10408398.2015.1126218.

### *Burdock* (**Arctium minus** *and* **A. lappa**)

"Burdock Root, Raw." FoodData Central. USDA Agricultural Research Service. https://fdc.nal.usda.gov/fdc-app.html#/food-details/169974/nutrients.

Li, Dandan, Jin M. Kim, Zhengyu Jin, and Jie Zhou. "Prebiotic Effectiveness of Inulin Extracted from Edible Burdock." *Anaerobe* 14, no. 1 (February 2008): 29–34. https://doi.org/10.1016/j.anaerobe.2007.10.002.

### *Ginkgo* (**Ginkgo biloba**)

"Ginkgo Nuts, Raw." FoodData Central. USDA Agricultural Research Service. https://fdc.nal.usda.gov/index.html.

Renshaw, Jarrett. "No Flowery Expressions: Easton Trees Just Reek." Themorningcall.com. December 27, 2018. www.mcall.com/news/mc-xpm-2008-04-24-4059169-story.html.

Zhang, Hong-Feng, Li-Bo Huang, Yan-Biao Zhong, Qi-Hui Zhou, Hui-Lin Wang, Guo-Qing Zheng, and Yan Lin. "An Overview of Systematic Reviews of *Ginkgo Biloba* Extracts for Mild Cognitive Impairment and Dementia." *Frontiers in Aging Neuroscience* 8 (December 6, 2016). https://doi.org/10.3389/fnagi.2016.00276.


### Grape / Wild Grape (Vitis *spp.*)

Bowen, Rebecca. "Conservation of Pennsylvania Native Wild Plants." Native Wild Plant Species Accounts. DCNR, March 2017. http://elibrary.dcnr.pa.gov/GetDocument?docId=1743381.

Liang, Zhenchang, Yingzhen Yang, Lailiang Cheng, and Gan-Yuan Zhong. "Polyphenolic Composition and Content in the Ripe Berries of Wild *Vitis* Species." *Food Chemistry* 132, no. 2 (May 15, 2012): 730–38. https://doi.org/10.1016/j.foodchem.2011.11.009.


### Ground Cherry (Physalis *spp.*)

Gibbons, Euell. *Stalking the Wild Asparagus*; with Illus. by Margaret F. Schroeder. New York, NY: D. McKay Co., 1962.

Kindscher, Kelly, Quinn Long, Steve Corbett, Kirsten Bosnak, Hillary Loring, Mark Cohen, and Barbara N. Timmermann. "The Ethnobotany and Ethnopharmacology of Wild Tomatillos, *Physalis Longifolia* Nutt., and Related *Physalis* Species: A Review." *Economic Botany* 66, no. 3 (September 5, 2012): 298–310. https://doi.org/10.1007/s12231-012-9210-7.

Ramadan, Mohamed Fawzy. "Bioactive Phytochemicals, Nutritional Value, and Functional Properties of Cape Gooseberry (*Physalis peruviana*): An Overview." *Food Research International* 44, no. 7 (August 2011): 1830–36. https://doi.org/10.1016/j.foodres.2010.12.042.

Rodrigues, Eliseu, Ismael Ivan Rockenbach, Ciriele Cataneo, Luciano Valdemiro Gonzaga, Eduardo Sidinei Chaves, and Roseane Fett. "Minerals and Essential Fatty Acids of the Exotic Fruit *Physalis peruviana* L." *Ciência e Tecnologia de Alimentos* 29, no. 3 (2009): 642–45. https://doi.org/10.1590/s0101-20612009000300029.

### *Hackberry* (Celtis *spp.*)

"2020 NJ Official Big Tree Registry." NJDEP New Jersey Department of Environmental Protection (2020). www.state.nj.us/dep/parksandforests/forest/community/bigtree_registry.html.

Adovasio, J. M., J. D. Gunn, J. Donahue, and R. Stuckenrath. "Meadowcroft Rockshelter, 1977: An Overview." *American Antiquity* 43, no. 4 (October 1978): 632–51. https://doi.org/10.2307/279496.

Demır, Fikret, Hakan Doğan, Musa Özcan, and Haydar Haciseferoğullari. "Nutritional and Physical Properties of Hackberry (*Celtis australis* L.)." *Journal of Food Engineering* 54, no. 3 (September 2002): 241–47. https://doi.org/10.1016/s0260-8774(01)00210-2.

### *Hawthorn* (Crataegus *spp.*)

Guo, Ruoling, Max H Pittler, and Edzard Ernst. "Hawthorn Extract for Treating Chronic Heart Failure." *Cochrane Database of Systematic Reviews* (2008). https://doi.org/10.1002/14651858.cd005312.pub2.

Keser, Serhat, Sait Celik, Semra Turkoglu, Okkes Yilmaz, and Ismail Turkoglu. "The Investigation of Some Bioactive Compounds and Antioxidant Properties of Hawthorn (*Crataegus monogyna* subsp. *monogyna* Jacq.)." *Journal of Intercultural Ethnopharmacology* 3, no. 2 (May 23, 2014): 51. https://doi.org/10.5455/jice.20140120103320.

### *Oak / Acorn* (Quercus *spp.*)

Elansary, Hosam O., Agnieszka Szopa, Paweł Kubica, Halina Ekiert, Mohamed A. Mattar, Mohamed A. Al-Yafrasi, Diaa O. El-Ansary, Tarek K. Zin El-Abedin, and Kowiyou Yessoufou. "Polyphenol Profile and Pharmaceutical Potential of *Quercus* Spp. Bark Extracts." *Plants* 8, no. 11 (2019): 486. https://doi.org/10.3390/plants8110486.

Vinha, Ana F., João C. M. Barreira, Anabela S. G. Costa, and M. Beatriz P. P. Oliveira. "A New Age for *Quercus* spp. Fruits: Review on Nutritional and Phytochemical Composition and Related Biological Activities of Acorns." *Comprehensive Reviews in Food Science and Food Safety* 15, no. 6 (August 16, 2016): 947–81. https://doi.org/10.1111/1541-4337.12220.

### *Partridge Berry* (**Mitchella repens**)

Foster, Steven, and James A. Duke. *Peterson Field Guide to Medicinal Plants and Herbs of Eastern and Central North America.* Boston: Houghton Mifflin Harcourt, 2014.

Rindfleisch, J. Adam. *Integrative Medicine, Part I: Incorporating Complementary/ Alternative Modalities, An Issue of Primary Care Clinics in Office Practice.* E-book. Saunders, 2010.

### *Pawpaw* (**Asimina triloba**)

Nam, Jin-Sik, Hye-Lim Jang, and Young Ha Rhee. "Nutritional Compositions in Roots, Twigs, Leaves, Fruit Pulp, and Seeds from Pawpaw (*Asimina triloba* [L.] Dunal) Grown in Korea." *Journal of Applied Botany and Food Quality* 91, (February 11, 2018): 47–55. https://test.ojs.openagrar.de/index .php/JABFQ/article/view/8466.

Pomper, Kirk. Rep. *Acetogenin Update* (2011). http://kysu.edu/wp-content/ uploads/2017/10/AcetoUpdate3.pdf.

Potts, Lisa F., Scott C. Smith, Michal Hetman, Pierre Champy, and Irene Litvan. "Annonacin in *Asimina triloba* Fruit: Implication for Neurotoxicity." *NeuroToxicology* 33, no. 1 (January 2012): 53–58. https://doi.org/10.1016/j .neuro.2011.10.009.

### *Persimmon* (**Diospyros virginiana**)

Hamel, Paul B., and Mary U. Chiltoskey. *Cherokee Plants and Their Uses: A 400 Year History.* Sylva, NC: Herald Publishing, 1975.

Homnava, A., J. Payne, P. Koehler, and R. Eitenmiller. "Provitamin A (Alpha-Carotene, Beta-Carotene, and Beta-Cryptoxanthin) and Ascorbic Acid Content of Japanese and American Persimmons." *Journal of Food Quality* 13, no. 2 (1990): 85–95. https://doi.org/10.1111/j.1745-4557.1990. tb00009.x.

Kobayashi, Hideki, George Antonious, and Kirk Pomper. "Phenolic Content and Antioxidant Capacity of American Persimmon (*Diospyros virginiana* L.) Teas." J Am Pom Soc. (APS) 71, no.2 (2017): 91–96. www.pubhort.org/ aps/71/v71_n2_a3.htm.

### Rose (**Rosa** *spp.*)

Mármol, Inés, Cristina Sánchez-De-Diego, Nerea Jiménez-Moreno, Carmen Ancín-Azpilicueta, and María Rodríguez-Yoldi. "Therapeutic Applications of Rose Hips from Different *Rosa* Species." *International Journal of Molecular Sciences* 18, no. 6 (2017): 1137. https://doi.org/10.3390/ijms18061137.


### Spicebush (**Lindera benzoin**)

Heisey, R. M., and Bernadette K. Gorham. "Antimicrobial Effects of Plant Extracts on *Streptococcus mutans*, *Candida albicans*, *Trichophyton rubrum* and Other Micro-Organisms." *Letters in Applied Microbiology* 14, no. 4 (April 1992): 136–39. https://doi.org/10.1111/j.1472-765x.1992.tb00668.x.

Setzer, William N. "The Phytochemistry of Cherokee Aromatic Medicinal Plants." *Medicines* 5, no. 4 (2018): 121. https://doi.org/10.3390/medicines5040121.


### Staghorn Sumac (**Rhus typhina**)

Kossah, Rima, Consolate Nsabimana, Jianxin Zhao, Haiqin Chen, Fengwei Tian, Hao Zhang, and Wei Chen. "Comparative Study on the Chemical Composition of Syrian Sumac (*Rhus coriaria* L.) and Chinese Sumac (*Rhus typhina* L.) Fruits." *Pakistan Journal of Nutrition* 8, no. 10 (January 2009): 1570–74. https://doi.org/10.3923/pjn.2009.1570.1574.


### Wintergreen (**Gaultheria procumbens**)

Michel, Piotr, Anna Dobrowolska, Agnieszka Kicel, Aleksandra Owczarek, Agnieszka Bazylko, Sebastian Granica, Jakub Piwowarski, and Monika Olszewska. "Polyphenolic Profile, Antioxidant and Anti-Inflammatory Activity of Eastern Teaberry (*Gaultheria procumbens* L.) Leaf Extracts." *Molecules* 19, no. 12 (August 2014): 20498–520. https://doi.org/10.3390/molecules191220498.

Ribnicky, David M., Alexander Poulev, and Ilya Raskin. "The Determination of Salicylates in *Gaultheria procumbens* for Use as a Natural Aspirin Alternative." *Journal of Nutraceuticals, Functional & Medical Foods* 4, no. 1 (2003): 39–52. https://doi.org/10.1300/j133v04n01_05.

## Mushrooms

### *Chanterelles* (**Cantharellus** *spp.*)

Drewnowska, Małgorzata, and Jerzy Falandysz. "Investigation on Mineral Composition and Accumulation by Popular Edible Mushroom Common Chanterelle (*Cantharellus cibarius*)." *Ecotoxicology and Environmental Safety* 113 (March 2015): 9–17. https://doi.org/10.1016/j.ecoenv.2014.11.028.

Keyhani, Jacqueline, and Ezzatollah Keyhani. "Polyphenol Oxidase in Golden Chanterelle (*Cantharellus cibarius*) Mushroom." *Microorganisms in Industry and Environment* (2010). https://doi.org/10.1142/9789814322119_0025.

Watanabe, Fumio, Joachi Schwarz, Shigeo Takenaka, Emi Miyamoto, Noriharu Ohishi, Esther Nelle, Rahel Hochstrasser, and Yukinori Yabuta. "Characterization of Vitamin B12 Compounds in the Wild Edible Mushrooms Black Trumpet (*Craterellus cornucopioides*) and Golden Chanterelle (*Cantharellus cibarius*)." *Journal of Nutritional Science and Vitaminology* 58, no. 6 (2012): 438–41. https://doi.org/10.3177/jnsv.58.438.

### *Chicken of the Woods* (**Laetiporus sulphureus**)

Khatua, Somanjana, Sandipta Ghosh, and Krishnendu Acharya. "*Laetiporus sulphureus* (Bull.: Fr.) Murr. as Food as Medicine." *Pharmacognosy Journal* 9, no. 6s (2017). https://doi.org/10.5530/pj.2017.6s.151.

### *Giant Puffball* (**Calvatia gigantea**)

Burk, William R. "Puffball Usages Among North American Indians." *Journal of Ethnobiology* 3, 1 (May 1983): 55–62. https://ethnobiology.org/sites/default/files/pdfs/JoE/3-1/Burk1983.pdf.

Chatterjee, Soumya, and Gunjan Biswas. "Antineoplastic Effect of Mushrooms: A Review." *Australian Journal of Crop Science* 5, 7 (July 2011): 904–11. www.researchgate.net/publication/259479127_Antineoplastic_effect_of_mushrooms_A_review.

Eroğlu, Canan, Mücahit Seçme, Pelin Atmaca, Oğuzhan Kaygusuz, Kutret Gezer, Gülseren Bağcı, and Yavuz Dodurga. "Extract of *Calvatia gigantea* Inhibits Proliferation of A549 Human Lung Cancer Cells." *Cytotechnology* 68, no. 5 (January 28, 2016): 2075–81. https://doi.org/10.1007/s10616-016-9947-4.

### Hen of the Woods (Grifola frondosa)

Konno, S., D. G. Tortorelis, S. A. Fullerton, A. A. Samadi, J. Hettiarachchi, and H. Tazaki. "A Possible Hypoglycaemic Effect of *Maitake* Mushroom on Type 2 Diabetic Patients." *Diabetic Medicine* 18, no. 12 (December 20, 2001): 1010–10. https://doi.org/10.1046/j.1464-5491.2001.00532-5.x.

Yeh, Jan-Ying, Li-Hui Hsieh, Kaun-Tzer Wu, and Cheng-Fang Tsai. "Antioxidant Properties and Antioxidant Compounds of Various Extracts from the Edible Basidiomycete *Grifola frondosa* (*Maitake*)." *Molecules* 16, no. 4 (April 15, 2011): 3197–3211. https://doi.org/10.3390/molecules16043197.

### Lion's Mane (Hericium erinaceus)

Cheung, P. C. K. "The Nutritional and Health Benefits of Mushrooms." *Nutrition Bulletin* 35, no. 4 (November 19, 2010): 292–99. https://doi.org/10.1111/j.1467-3010.2010.01859.x.

Mori, Koichiro, Satoshi Inatomi, Kenzi Ouchi, Yoshihito Azumi, and Takashi Tuchida. "Improving Effects of the Mushroom Yamabushitake (*Hericium erinaceus*) on Mild Cognitive Impairment: A Double-Blind Placebo-Controlled Clinical Trial." *Phytotherapy Research* 23, no. 3 (June 2009): 367–72. https://doi.org/10.1002/ptr.2634.

### Morels (Morchella *spp.*)

Ajmal, Maryam, Abida Akram, Anum Ara, Shaista Akhund, and Brian Gagosh Nayyar. "*Morchella esculenta*: An Edible and Health Beneficial Mushroom." *Pakistan Journal of Food Sciences* 25, no. 2 (2015): 71–78. https://pdfs.semanticscholar.org/55ab/16357ab129f9f770896e73676e28f7a9b438.pdf.

### Pheasant's Back (Polyporus squamosus)

Bulam, Sanem, Nebahat Şule Üstün, and Aysun Pekşen. "*Polyporus squamosus* (Huds.) Fr. in the Black Sea Region." *Turkish Journal of Agriculture—Food Science and Technology* 6, no. 2 (2018): 183. https://doi.org/10.24925/turjaf.v6i2.183-188.1546.

# GLOSSARY

**Aggregate fruit**—A fruit that consists of a number of small fruits.

**Alternate leaves**—Leaves that are not directly across from each other on the stem.

**Anthelmintic**—A substance that destroys parasitic worms in the body.

**Anthocyanins**—Red and purple plant pigments that act as antioxidants.

**Anti-inflammatory**—A substance that reduces inflammation or swelling.

**Antimicrobial**—An agent that acts against bacteria, viruses, and fungi.

**Antioxidant**—A substance that prevents or slows cellular damage caused by free radicals.

**Basal leaves**—Leaves at the base of a plant.

**Biennial**—A plant that completes its life cycle in two years.

**Bract**—A modified leaf.

**Brambles**—Members of the *Rubus* genus, bearing aggregate fruit and thorns.

**Compound leaves**—Those composed of several leaflets on one stem.

**Corm**—Underground plant part similar to a bulb but lacking layered scales.

**Deciduous**—A tree or shrub that sheds its leaves in the fall.

**Drupe**—A fruit that contains a single seed.

**Entire**—Leaves having no teeth or lobes.

**Flavonoids**—A large group of plant compounds that have antioxidant and anti-inflammatory health benefits.

**Flavonols**—A subcategory of flavonoids found in plant foods.

**Foliage**—Plant leaves.

**Free radicals**—Unstable molecules in the body that are responsible for cell damage, accelerated aging, and disease.

**Genus**—A group of related species.

**Gills**—Paper-thin flaps under the cap of some mushroom species; they produce the spores.

**Herbaceous**—Plants that have nonwoody stems.

**Hirsutism**—Excess facial and body hair.

**Hybridize**—Crossbreeding of two different species or varieties.

**Immunomodulatory**—Having the ability to affect immune functions.

**Invasive species**—An organism that is not native to an ecosystem and usually causes harm.

**Latex**—A substance produced by many plants in response to physical damage.

**Lenticels**—Breathing pores responsible for gas exchange.

**Mushroom**—A spore-producing fruiting body of a fungus.

**Mycorrhizal**—Mushrooms that form an underground network of fine threads connecting with tree roots. The two organisms share nutrients.

**Naturalized**—A species of foreign origin that adapts and spreads in its new location.

**Oxalates (oxalic acid)**—Plant compounds that can bind with calcium, making it unavailable to the body.

**Palmate**—Having three or more parts radiating out from a common point.

**Panicle**—A branching cluster of flowers that grows on the end of a stem.

**Pemmican**—A mixture of dried fruit, animal fat, and meat made by Native American tribes. It provided a concentrated source of calories and protein.

**Perennial**—A plant that lives more than two years.

**Petiole**—The stalk that attaches a leaf to the plant stem.

**Phenolic compounds / phenolics**—A group of compounds found in fruits and vegetables that have antioxidant properties and are health-protective.

**Pinnate**—Having leaflets arranged on each side of the main stalk.

**Plant shoots**—The new growth of a plant that gives rise to stems and leaves.

**Pollen**—Powderlike grains that contain the male reproductive cells of a plant.

**Polyphenols**—Beneficial plant substances that can help prevent disease.

**Polypore**—A type of mushroom that has pores or tubes on its underside.

**Pores**—The ends of tubes within a mushroom cap that appear as tiny holes on the cap underside.

**Rhizome**—A plant stem that grows horizontally under the ground and produces roots.

**Rosette**—A circular arrangement of leaves that radiate from a short stem at ground level.

**Samara**—A winged seed designed to be carried by the wind.

**Saponins**—A category of naturally occurring plant chemicals that have soap-like qualities. They may have adverse or beneficial health effects.

**Scurvy**—Vitamin C deficiency disease.

**Simple leaf**—A leaf that is not divided into smaller leaflets.

**Species**—A group of organisms that have similar characteristics and are capable of interbreeding.

**Spring ephemeral**—A plant that produces flowers and seeds to complete its life cycle in spring.

**Understory**—The layer of vegetation below a forest canopy.

**Whorl**—A set of at least three leaves that radiate from a point and wrap around a stem.

**Winter annuals**—Plants that germinate in the fall, survive the winter, then continue growth in spring to complete the life cycle before dying back when hot weather arrives.

# INDEX

*Acer* spp., 53–55
acorn, 193–96
*Alliaria petiolata,* 34–37
*Allium tricoccum,* 68–71
*Allium vineale,* 92–95
*Amelanchier* spp., 145–47
*Arctium lappa,* 172–74
*Arctium* spp., 172–74
*Asclepias syriaca,* 112–15
*Asimina triloba,* 200–202
autumn olive, 161–63

*Barbarea vulgaris,* 96–98
beach plum, 100–102
bedstraw, 16
beech, 164–67
bittercress, 42–45, 88
black raspberry, 110
blackberry, 109–11
black cherry, 103–5
black locust, 2–4
black trumpet mushroom, 225
black walnut, 168–71
blueberry, 106–8
brambles, 109–11
burdock, 172–74
butternut, 171

*Calvatia gigantea,* 230–32
*Cantharellus* spp., 222–25
*Cardamine hirsuta,* 42–45
catbrier, 38
cattail, 5–8
*Celtis* spp., 186–88
*Cercis canadensis,* 72–74
*Cerioporus squamosus,* 244
chanterelles, 222–25
*Chenopodium album,* 125–27
chicken of the woods, 226–29
chickweed, 9–11
chicory, 12–15
*Cichorium intybus,* 12–15
*Claytonia virginica,* 75–78
clearweed, 83
cleavers, 16–18
clover, 159
common milkweed, 112–15

cornelian cherry, 116–18
*Cornus mas,* 116–18
*Crataegus* spp., 189–92
*Craterellus fallax,* 225
creeping Charlie, 37, 48
curly dock, 19–22

dame's rocket, 23–25
dandelion, 26–29
*Daucus carota,* 141–44
dewberry, 109, 111
*Diospyros virginiana,* 203–5
dock, 19, 21–22
dryad's saddle, 244, 246

eastern redbud, 72, 74
eastern white pine, 30–33
*Elaeagnus umbellata,* 161–63
elderberry, 119–21
*Erythronium americanum,* 86–88

*Fagus grandifolia,* 164–67
fairy spuds, 75, 76, 77
field garlic, 92
*Fragaria virginiana,* 151–53

*Galium aparine,* 16–18
garlic mustard, 34–37
*Gaultheria procumbens,* 217–20
giant puffball, 230–32
ginkgo, 175–78
*Ginkgo biloba,* 175–78
*Glechoma hederacea,* 37, 48, 66
grape, 179–82
greenbrier, 38–41
*Grifola frondosa,* 233–35
ground cherry, 183–85

hackberry, 186–88
hairy bittercress, 42–45
hawthorn, 189–92
heal-all, 122–24
hen of the woods, 233–35
henbit, 46–48
*Hericium erinaceus,* 236–38
*Hesperis matronalis,* 23–25

Japanese knotweed, 49–52
*Juglans cinerea,* 171
*Juglans nigra,* 168–71

kousa dogwood, 118

*Laetiporus cincinnatus,* 229
*Laetiporus sulphureus,* 226–29
lamb's-quarter, 125–27
*Lamium amplexicaule,* 46–48
*Lamium purpureum,* 64–67
*Laportea canadensis,* 83
*Leucanthemum vulgare,* 135–37
*Lindera benzoin,* 210–12
lion's mane, 236–38

*Maitake,* 233, 235
maple, 53–55
*Matteuccia struthiopteris,* 56–59
mayapple, 128–30
*Mentha spicata,* 148–50
milkweed, 112–15
*Mitchella repens,* 197–99
mock strawberry, 152–53
*Morchella* spp., 239–43
morels, 239–43
*Morus* spp., 131–34
mulberry, 131–34

*Nasturtium officinale,* 154–56

oak, 193–96
ostrich fern, 56–59
*Oxalis stricta,* 157–59
oxeye daisy, 135–37

partridge berry, 197–99
pawpaw, 200–202
persimmon, 203–5
pheasant's back, 244–47
phlox, 24
*Physalis* spp., 183–85
*Picea* spp., 79–81
*Pilea pumila,* 83
pine, 30–32, 223
*Pinus strobus,* 30–33
plantain, 60–63
*Plantago* spp., 60–63
*Podophyllum peltatum,* 128–30
*Polygonum cuspidatum,* 49–52

*Polyporus squamosus,* 244–47
*Portulaca oleracea,* 138–40
*Potentilla indica,* 152
*Prunella vulgaris,* 122–24
*Prunus maritima,* 100–102
*Prunus serotina,* 103–5
purple deadnettle, 64–67
purslane, 138–40

Queen Anne's lace, 141–44
*Quercus* spp., 193–96

ramps, 68–71
raspberry, 107, 109–11
redbud, 72–74
*Rhus typhina,* 213–16
*Robinia pseudoacacia,* 2–4
*Rosa* spp., 206–9
rose, 206–9
*Rubus* spp., 109–11
*Rumex acetosella,* 159
*Rumex crispus,* 19–22
Russian olive, 163

*Sambucus* spp., 119–21
self-heal, 122
serviceberry, 108, 145–47
sheep sorrel, 159
*Smilax rotundifolia,* 38–41
sourgrass, 157
spearmint, 148–50
spicebush, 210–12
spring beauty, 75–78
spruce, 79–81
staghorn sumac, 213–16
*Stellaria media,* 9–11
stinging nettle, 82–85
strawberry, 151–53
sulphur shelf, 226
sumac, 213–15

*Taraxacum officinale,* 26–29
teaberry, 217–19
*Trifolium* spp., 159
trout lily, 86–88
*Typha* spp., 5–8

*Urtica dioica,* 82–85

*Vaccinium* spp., 106–8

*Viola* spp., 89–91
violets, 89–91
*Vitis* spp., 179–82

watercress, 24, 44, 98, 154–56
white pine, 30–33
wild carrot, 141–44
wild garlic, 92–95

wineberry, 109, 110
wintercress, 96–98
wintergreen, 199, 217–20
wood nettle, 83
wood sorrel, 157–59

yellow dock, 19